Happiness:
A New Perspective

For Jo, Emma, Marsha,
Nick and Laura

Contents

1

Introduction

In the spring of 1790, Xavier de Maistre, a twenty-seven-year-old Frenchman, embarked upon an expedition, but unlike contemporary explorers he was not bound for the fantastic jungles of South America or the exotic islands of the South Pacific – he planned to circumnavigate his bedroom. In *A Journey Around My Room* this eccentric man explains how he used his armchair to teeter from one wall to another before scaling his bed and forging a route to his desk. All the time he enquired of and admired objects he had previously ignored; he delighted in the colour of his bedding and regarded his mirror as 'one of the marvels of the country through which I am strolling'.[1]

While Xavier's voyage, which he recommended to the price conscious traveller as well as those afraid of storms and robbers, might initially seem rather bizarre, he actually made a profound insight: 'That the pleasure we derive from journeys is perhaps dependent more on the mindset with which we travel than on the destination we travel to'.[2] He shows us that enjoying your surroundings relies much more on how you view them than on what they are. By altering his outlook, he was able to feel as much wonder when surveying his room as another person might feel when gazing at a majestic view from the top of a mountain. In a similar manner, this book will argue that anyone can become happier by changing their perspective rather than the conditions of their life.

A new approach to attaining happiness is certainly needed: over the last fifty years, despite great economic progress, there has been almost no increase in average happiness in the economically developed countries.[3] Indeed, depression is now ten times as prevalent as it was in 1960.[4] Some commentators argue that the social problems which have accompanied economic progress are to blame: increasing divorce rates, longer commutes, high crime rates, declining church attendance, decreasing trust within communities and addiction to television are all commonly put forward as causes of Western angst. Although there may be some truth in these claims, it seems doubtful that we will ever resolve these issues or, even if we could, that doing so would lead to a future utopia. There will always be social problems in one form or another and, while helping solve them may be a laudable aim, taking responsibility for your own happiness seems a more plausible route to increasing it than waiting for social reform to do so.

As such, the first underlying argument of this book is that individuals living in wealthy democratic countries do not need to seek to change society or their lifestyles in order to become happier. Most of us possess the raw materials for living a happy, rewarding life and need to change our perspectives, rather than our life circumstances, in order to realise that ambition. But doing so is not easy. Consequently, this book will explain both why it is so difficult to alter your outlook and recommend ways to overcome these obstacles.

The other central argument of this book is that developing a deeper understanding of what happiness means is necessary in order to appreciate how it might better be obtained. Many self-help books on positive emotion distinguish between different types of happiness and these distinctions are useful in terms of understanding both what happiness is and how it can be obtained. Typically, there are two types of happiness put forward – a first type consisting of momentary feelings, such as joy and pleasure, and a second type which comprises a more general feeling of long-term well-being (e.g. contentment and satisfaction over a period of time). Philosophers also talk of a third type of happiness, however, which involves a sense that your life is meaningful – that it has some value beyond pleasurable sensations or being content which does not necessarily involve any felt emotion. Of the self-help writers who do mention this kind of happiness none go on to explain how we might attain it.[5] Clearly religion offers one such route, but if you are an agnostic, an atheist or have doubts in your faith, where do you turn? In such a subjective area it is impossible to provide anything like a definitive answer, but chapters 6 and 7 lay out one way of working through the problem with the hope that readers can use the method described as a guide to discern their own opinions. Up to chapter 6 the focus will be on increasing types one and two happiness. Only by combining the findings of psychologists with the enquiries of philosophy can we truly understand what it means to be happy. The resulting discussion ranges from evolutionary psychology to crime statistics and includes some of the most fundamental questions we can ask about existence and ourselves.

As well as the content, the approach of this book is different to most self-help publications, a large number of which fail their readers. They offer visions of unbridled success and promise the hope of a perfect future which only leads to feelings of inadequacy and dissatisfaction when mere mortals inevitably fail to become the richest, thinnest, most popular person in the world. Anecdotes and cliched quotes are frequently used as the main evidence to back up their claims and many of the recommended exercises are impractical and tiresome.

This book, by contrast, is built on four premises:

1. There will be no exercises and the advice given will be practical. Because humans vary so much, specific guidance is never going to produce the same results in everyone. General guidelines, though, can be of use and will be included.

2. In an age overflowing with information, brevity is a virtue. As such, this book aims to be concise.

3. Advice will be sensible about how much happier you can realistically become. It is pretty obvious that some individuals are naturally more upbeat than others and, indeed, some people actively enjoy having a bit of a whinge every so often. It is not for me to tell you how happy you should be or to make you feel that you have to go around smiling all the time. Please receive what is said in the spirit in which it is intended – friendly and well-meaning, not prescriptive and dictatorial.

4. Scientific evidence will form the basis of advice as much as possible, rather than relying on the untested testimony of a single individual. The personal stories found in many self-help books are often remarkable and powerful but they provide only one example. Hundreds of people caught in the same circumstances might react completely differently. Only by relying upon evidence gathered in scientific experiments can we hope to understand whether a particular suggestion is likely to work for the majority of people, rather than assuming that just because one person found it useful we all will (for more information about the scientific study of happiness see the appendix).

Finally, while this book's suggestions are based upon scientific evidence, please remember that they are just that – suggestions. Some of them may work for you, others may not. The only way you will know, though, is if you give them a go. Before we look at examples of how to increase happiness, however, we first need to understand the obstacles that stand in our way.

2

Obstacles to Greater Happiness

Feeling happier over a sustained period of time is no easy feat; if it were, you would not be reading this book. To better enable us to achieve increased levels of happiness types one and two we first need to understand the obstacles that stand in our way. What can prevent us from becoming happier? How much of a hindrance are our genes? Why is it that people say money cannot buy happiness? Only by answering questions such as these will we be able to find the strategies which are most likely to succeed. As we shall see, some barriers to greater happiness have only begun to be understood relatively recently, while other factors that are widely regarded as impediments to happiness are not really obstacles at all. What follows is by no means a complete list – it is more of a selection of factors that are important to understand at this point in the discussion. Of these, perhaps the most critical issue to address is how much we can hope to influence our own happiness.

Genes

More specifically, to what extent do our genes determine our natural predisposition to feeling positive or negative? It has long been recognised that some people are naturally more upbeat than others. This observation has led to the claim that there is hardly anything we can do to change our happiness. Some people, it is argued, can suffer nothing but setbacks and always remain cheerful while others stay glum no matter how fortunate they are. There is certainly an element of truth in this, but is there really nothing we can do to alter our emotional destiny?

Luckily surveys from identical twins separated at birth provide an encouraging answer. These studies have found that people with the same genes, despite different upbringings and life circumstances, have similar but, crucially, not identical happiness levels. Analysis of this data has led researchers to suggest that happiness is determined somewhere between 25-50% by a person's genes.[6] Therefore they only determine the *range* of happiness levels that a person is likely to be able to experience. As an illustration, let's imagine two individuals; sullen looking Gordon and his smiley friend Tony. On a 10-point scale of happiness Gordon may be naturally predisposed to an average of say 6 while Tony to 7. Despite this natural difference, however, each may be capable of moving 3 points up or down from that baseline, which means that if Gordon focused on the positive aspects of his life and consciously set out to enjoy it while Tony only ever paid attention to the negative, Gordon could actually end up being substantially happier than Tony. **We cannot alter our genes, but they do not have to determine the outcome of our lives.**

Adaptation

So our genes may represent only a partial obstacle to greater happiness. The next barrier we are going to discuss also involves something we are all (or at least most of us!) born with – a brain. In particular, we are going to investigate the impediments to happiness that are a result of the way the brain functions. In order to do this we have to understand why it operates as it does and, to make sense of that, we need to comprehend the environment in which it developed. That environment, according to the theory of evolution, was a primitive hunter-gatherer existence in which survival of oneself and ones genes was paramount.[7] It was under the huge uncertainties and pressures of this habitat that modern humans developed. Just as biologists can study how different elements of the human body evolved, evolutionary psychologists look at the way the mind behaves and attempt to decipher the primitive challenges different features of the brain evolved to overcome. A result of becoming stressed, for example, is an increase in heart rate, blood pressure and breathing rate, all of which would allow you to run away faster from an attacking lion.[8] What then, was the original function of happiness?

It is important to note that no emotion evolved to fulfil only one specific purpose; each emotion can serve multiple functions. Joy, for instance, can encourage us to engage in sexual reproduction, commune with friends, and consume food and drink amongst other things. Speaking generally, though, positive emotions tend to promote activities which would have benefited both your survival and your genes'. In the case of joy, sexual reproduction replicates your genes, making friends provides a potential support network if you are ill or attacked, and food and drink are obviously essential in order to remain alive. But you can have too much of a good thing; spend too long copulating with the Neolithic blonde with the shortest mammoth-skin skirt and you risk becoming too weak to hunt for prey. Happiness, or at least the prospect of it, encourages us to strive for survival benefits, but to enjoy those benefits for only a limited period of time. This ensures that we do not spend so long delighting in them that we ignore other factors vital for survival. In other words, the human brain is programmed to adapt so that, whatever good fortune befalls us, we never remain too happy for too long. Indeed, the undesirability of complete happiness is best summed up by the idea of delirium. To say that someone is delirious can mean that they are in a state of wild excitement and experiencing a feeling of ecstasy, but to remain delirious for a sustained period of time implies that a person has become delusional and mentally disturbed: while a degree of positive emotion is welcome, an excess is regarded as overwhelming.

A good example of adaptation in the modern world is seen when someone purchases an expensive luxury item. Frequently there is an emotional high associated with buying the item, but this feeling is usually relatively short lived and people return to their previous level of happiness soon afterwards. We adapt to the pleasure provided by the purchase and return to our previous level of happiness. This might make adaptation seem like rather a bad thing, but it also has a good side. It can enable us to return to our normal happiness level when we experience adverse events. In one study, for example, people with kidney disease who had to undergo up to nine hours of dialysis a week were found to be just as happy as a group of healthy subjects.[9] Adaptation can vary in speed and extent though. For reasons as yet unknown, although it is possible to have a reasonable guess, studies have found that people who experience widowhood or excessive noise pollution can take many years to adapt and often return to a level of happiness slightly below their original rating.[10]

It is worth noting, however, that short-term unhappy emotions evolved in us because they too served a useful survival function and, even though they can overreact in the modern world, they still have benefits. Mild worry, for instance, rehearses possible dangers which leaves you better placed to meet potential challenges. Although negative emotions that are deeply felt and persist for a long time can be damaging, without experiencing some temporary mood blips we might make decisions that are not in our long-term best interests. Indeed, without experience of what it feels like to be unhappy, one could never know what happiness is because there would be nothing to compare it against.

The evolutionary benefits of different emotions mean that everyone's happiness naturally varies throughout the day, with a study of 909 working women showing a pattern of positivity increasing during the morning until lunchtime, then decreasing mid-afternoon before rising again from late afternoon through to bedtime.[11] As a result, everyone is going to feel less happy at some point in the day. The purpose of the advice over the following chapters will not be to replace this pattern with one that shows a constant high level of happiness, if this is even possible. Instead, it will be to help you **find ways of adapting slightly slower to positive events and adapting slightly quicker to negative ones.**

Excessive Rumination

A key part of the latter is learning to deal with rumination. Many of us spend a good deal of our time analysing ourselves and assessing how we acted in various situations. Some reflection is beneficial, but numerous studies have found that too much rumination can reinforce rather than relieve feelings of anxiety, inadequacy and unhappiness.[12] Likewise, when we are wronged, hurt or injured by another person, most people feel angry or resentful. Such a reaction is understandable but usually relatively short-lived as the transgressions are either forgotten or forgiven. Feeling bitterness and vengeance towards someone for a prolonged period of time, however, can be a form of excessive rumination. Both personal observation and empirical evidence from psychology studies confirm that dwelling on such thoughts is emotionally draining and militates against happiness.[13] **A key element to feeling happier, therefore, is to develop strategies which restrain over-thinking and prolonged anger.** As with other personality traits, some will be more inclined naturally to excessive contemplation than others but most people should find at least part of the advice contained in the next chapter useful.

Wealth

A more debatable obstacle to happiness is wealth. One of the most popular statements about happiness is that money cannot buy it, yet many people feel they would be happier if they earned slightly more. Which is true? Our tendency to adapt to new circumstances and the fact that over the last fifty years there has been almost no increase in average happiness levels in the economically developed countries despite a huge rise in real (i.e. taking account of inflation) wages suggests that additional wealth has no lasting impact on happiness.[14] In the Western world this is largely true, but not so on a global scale. Studies of worldwide happiness have shown that, on average, wealthier nations tend to be happier than poorer ones.[15]

Most academics agree that this is not because wealth in itself makes people happier but because of the benefits it can confer on a group of people.[16] Economic development correlates with reduced crime, increased political freedom, better human rights and a reduction in the number of the impoverished. When these factors are at their worst they present a sizeable barrier to happiness. As such, improving the economies of the world's poorer countries is likely to increase happiness in these places. In the West, however, we are lucky to have low crime and poverty rates, combined with much political freedom and decent human rights. Of course each of these elements could still be improved, but they are currently good enough that improving them would not have a significant impact on happiness levels. This, combined with the evidence of adaptation, suggests that **focusing on economic progress in countries which are already well developed will not lead to higher levels of happiness.**

Sleep

Returning to Western society, it is often said that if we could all get more sleep we would be happier. Despite this claim, there has been surprisingly little research conducted on the relationship between happiness and sleep. There is, however, a large body of evidence which looks at how sleep affects tiredness. It seems reasonable to assume that feeling excessively tired will act against happiness. So how much sleep do researchers recommend? Most adults get 7-8 hours of sleep a night and there are some who claim this is insufficient. They argue that routinely getting 7-8 hours sleep a night leads to the build up of a large sleep debt which can only be masked over by consuming caffeine and other stimulants.[17] Our daily experience is held out as living proof of the problem; why else would we feel drowsy in the morning and tired by mid-afternoon? There are actually some very good reasons why we are less energetic at these times and they have nothing to do with sleep deprivation. There are no studies which show an increase in morning alertness among people who sleep longer.[18] Just as it takes a few minutes to get to sleep, so it also takes a few minutes to wake up properly. The reason you might feel more alert when you wake up after a Sunday morning lie-in compared to 7am on a Monday is that on Monday you probably use an alarm, whereas on Sunday you wake naturally. Jolting yourself suddenly out of sleep means it takes slightly longer for your body to adjust to being awake.

That afternoon dip in energy levels is also explicable. The typical person is at their most lethargic in the morning. Alertness rises sharply after breakfast and remains roughly constant until just after lunch when it declines, before increasing in the late afternoon, only reducing again when it is time for bed.[19] Extending our average sleeping time from 7-8 hours per night to 8-9 hours can eliminate the mid-afternoon lull, but this is not an indication that we are chronically sleep deprived.[20] This dip is perfectly natural – it is probably an evolutionary hangover from the disposition of our equatorial ancestors to take a nap when the sun's heat was at its peak and exertion was inefficient. As such, we should not be overly worried with how to overcome it. Indeed, there is some evidence that people who sleep 7-8 hours a night are less prone to health complaints and live longer than those having more sleep.[21] If you do find that you are significantly less happy during the afternoon, though, as an alternative to sleeping longer you could try taking a nap, if working habits permit, or consuming a small quantity of caffeine. The diminutive nature of the afternoon dip in alertness, however, is unlikely to cause a sizeable shift in mood for most people.

The possibility of long-term sleep debt is also a highly debatable issue.[22] Yes we might need some extra sleep if we get less than 6 hours rest, but our bodies do not build up a permanent sleep deficit which we need to repay before we can be healthy. When Randy Gardner stayed awake for 264 hours (11 days!) continuously in 1964, he only needed to regain a quarter of the sleep he had lost before he returned to normal and subsequent sleep deprivation experiments have produced similar results.[23] Unlike your local bank, the brain seems far more benevolent with its debts; as long as part is repaid, the balance is scrapped.

Obviously we are liable to become crotchety if we get significantly less sleep than normal and every person has a slightly different optimum level of sleep. Indeed, the very young and elderly have quite different sleep requirements than the average adult. It is also true that shift workers suffer sleep loss as a result of regularly altering their sleeping patterns. The important point, though, is that **for the vast majority of people, getting 7-8 hours sleep a night is sufficient.** You may find it enjoyable to sleep for longer but, in much the same way as you might take pleasure in eating more food than you strictly need, it is not a necessity.

Diet

If we do not need more sleep to feel happier, what about our diets? How much attention should we pay to what we eat? Diet is certainly discussed a lot by the press – barely a week seems to go by without some new food revelation. Crisps may cause cancer, but on the plus side fish oils could improve my intelligence and the anti-ageing benefits of pomegranates might help counteract those dangerous fried potatoes.[24] The media also regularly announce the discovery of 'happy' foods. These foods, so the theory often goes, contain unusually high concentrations of nutrients which are supposed to promote happiness. What is the truth? Will eating these foods really increase your happiness?

The problem with much of this nutritional advice is that it is frequently based on a single study (although many others may contradict its findings), or an incredible extrapolation from quite mundane findings, or research conducted on animals with no evidence for any effect on humans whatsoever. Even when a number of experiments appear to support the same conclusion, weaknesses in the methods used may invalidate the results. Faced with such pitfalls, Ben Goldacre, a doctor, concludes that when claims are made about diet and health 'anyone who ever expresses anything with certainty is basically wrong, because the evidence for cause and effect in this area is almost always weak and circumstantial'.[25]

This is not to say that we should ignore all dietary advice – recommendations to decrease our salt, sugar and saturated fat intakes while eating more fruits and vegetables rest on much firmer scientific evidence.[26] Indeed, eating a balanced diet is essential for promoting health. The point, though, is that unlike this general advice, specific claims about the effects of individual foods rest on flimsy evidence and are best ignored. There is no need to be scaremongered into hunting out 'super foods' and disregarding perfectly good ingredients.

Having said this, well-conducted experiments involving nutritional supplements given to prisoners have shown a significant effect on behaviour and mood. The participants who reacted most strongly to the supplements, though, were those who had the worst diets and therefore were lacking essential nutrients. It is true that some people do suffer from a natural deficiency in chemicals that promote happiness, but for the vast majority of people eating a balanced diet is all that is needed to promote happiness. This is why official advice is that 'most people can get all of the nutrients they need from a balanced diet and do not need dietary supplements'.[27] Indeed, considering the health benefits claimed by many nutrition pill manufacturers for their products, it is rather ironic that consuming too much of certain vitamins and minerals is regarded by authoritative sources as potentially damaging to ones health.[28]

In conclusion, while many of us are accustomed to being irritable if we go without food for too long or noticing our energy levels peak and then trough after a sugar binge, little more than preliminary studies have been conducted to study the effects of individual nutrients on mood. Scientists have been able to make the general conclusion that **a balanced diet promotes mental well-being** but when someone makes a specific claim for a certain nutrient be very suspicious.[29] If you want a diet that is healthy both physically and mentally, eat moderate portions, consume a variety of foods (including a range of fruits and vegetables) and use fresh produce as much as possible – that's it.[30]

Summary

This chapter has sought to understand some of the factors that can prevent people from feeling happier. We have seen that in Western society we should not be overly concerned with becoming wealthier, sleeping longer or eating anything other than a balanced diet. Rather, as our genes only partially determine our happiness levels, a key to becoming happier is learning how to slow adaptation to positive events and speed adaptation to negative ones (a central element of which is knowing how to prevent excessive rumination). It is important to note that other barriers to happiness involving work and relationships have not been discussed because they are large enough areas to demand separate consideration (chapters 4 and 5). Before turning to them, though, we will look at techniques designed to overcome the problems of adaptation and excessive worry.

3
Changing Perspective

Have you ever returned from a holiday where the food was terrible and found yourself delighting in the taste of a simple home-cooked meal? Or discovered a new appreciation for the everyday comforts of home after a wet camping trip? Such events are rare, but the change in perspective frequently results in a temporary mood boost. One purpose of this chapter is to explain how we might experience happiness boosts like these more often and sustain them for longer. The other is to suggest ways of overcoming negative emotions faster. By using a combination of approaches we can make enduring adjustments to how we see different elements of our lives and hopefully become lastingly happier as a result.

Avoiding Repetition

To get us started it will be helpful to look at a couple of experiments. In the first, participants were split into three groups. One group were asked to make a record once a week of five things for which they were thankful and to do so for ten weeks. The second group were asked to do the same but instead to record five hassles, while the third group were asked to note five major events. At the end of the experiment the first group were found to be more optimistic and more satisfied with their lives than the others because, unlike the others, they had been consciously appreciating life.[31]

From this evidence it would be easy to draw the simple conclusion that to increase happiness all we need do is find ways to appreciate life more. There is an important qualification to this suggestion, however, which a different study highlights. This time participants were asked to write down five things for which they were grateful. Half of them were told to do so once a week and the other half to do so three times a week. Interestingly, after six weeks, those who had recorded their gratitude only once a week showed greater improvements in happiness than those who had done so three times a week.[32]

Based on the findings of chapter 2 we can guess why – the three-times-a-week group adapted to the benefits of expressing thankfulness. By repeating the same exercise too frequently they ceased to derive any positive emotion from the exercise. Instead it became boring, mundane and a chore. We have all experienced similar habituation when, for example, we recover from a nasty illness and feel enraptured by life for a day or so before returning to a more normal level of emotion. As St Augustine noted over a thousand years ago, 'Daily familiarity gradually blunts the edge of wonder.'[33]

Experiments and personal experience teach us that if we are to become lastingly happier we need to find ways of preventing adaptation, or at least altering the rate at which it occurs. How are we to do so? One tactic, as the second experiment shows, is to avoid savouring the same stimuli too frequently. Enjoy a good chocolate bar, but perhaps not every day. Having said this, people adapt to positive experiences at different rates, so it is only through experience that you can determine how much is too much.

What can we do, though, if we have no choice but to perform the same activity repeatedly? In this situation we might try to vary the way we go about it in order to keep it fresh and stimulating. Take the daily commute to work as an example. I used to walk down Fleet Street in London every day to get to work. Usually I would keep to the right-hand side of the road and scurry along to reach my office as quickly as possible. One day, however, roadworks forced me to take an alternative route and I had to walk along the left-hand pavement. As I did so I noticed things I had never seen before – an Art Deco clock attached to one building, a decorative pedestal on another. I also saw familiar things in an unfamiliar light, so for the first time I really appreciated the beauty of the steeple adorning St Bride's church. If simply crossing the road had the power to transform my daily commute from dreary drudgery into something quite pleasant, imagine how much more there would be to experience by exploring the many possible routes I could take.

One final tip on ways to hinder adaptation to positive emotions is to find as many happiness inducing activities as possible and vary them frequently. By doing so we not only benefit from several different experiences, we also prevent ourselves from overindulging in just one.

Savouring

Everyone will obviously already have certain activities that they enjoy and you are capable yourself of discovering things to add to your list. An often overlooked but rich source of positive emotions, however, is offered by taking greater joy in the simple activities of daily life. As such, it is worth looking at different techniques designed to encourage finding more happiness in everyday experience.

Buddhists, for example, have long found benefit in savouring the present through a practice they refer to as mindfulness. Thich Nhat Hanh, one of the pre-eminent modern Buddhist writers on mindfulness, recommends that when we engage in apparently mundane activities we take our time over them and appreciate the things we would normally fail to notice. For instance, when washing dishes:

> Once you are standing in front of the sink with ... your hands in the water, it really is quite pleasant. I enjoy taking my time with each dish, being fully aware of the dish, the water and each movement of my hands. I know that if I hurry in order to eat dessert sooner, the time of washing dishes will be unpleasant and not worth living. That would be a pity, for each minute, each second of life is a miracle.

When eating a tangerine, Thich recommends you peel it slowly, notice 'the fragrance ... and then bring it up to [your] mouth and have a mindful bite, in full awareness of the texture and taste of the fruit and the juice. ... Take your time eating a tangerine.'[34] In such moments our attention is wholly focused on the object in question and we block out all distractions. In doing so we recognise the value of that particular experience.

Another technique to encourage gratitude for life's gifts is to imagine what it would be like to die or lose someone close to you – in effect, to say to yourself, 'Today may be my last, let me appreciate all that it contains.' Although you might be young and healthy, death is a constant, although remote, possibility. Indeed, as terrible as it may seem, there is always the chance that someone close to you might die before you see them again or that you may suffer serious injuries in an accident. Recognising the possibility of such undesirable events is not to promote worry but to make one conscious of the value of what is present now. Obviously it would be impractical to live each day as if it were our last: to be conscious of the fact that it *could* be our last, however, reminds us that **nothing should be taken for granted.**

An alternative way to be thankful for what you have is to focus on positive events from the past. An interesting study showed that reminiscing about happy events led participants to feel more positive about their present lives.[35] By reflecting on good past experiences they boosted their self-esteem and recognised how fortunate they were to have such moments. Be wary that when looking back there is a danger of contrasting previous bliss with present dissatisfaction. The purpose of reflection should not be to find fault with your current situation but to celebrate the enjoyment you have experienced.

Finally, many people find that one of the benefits of undertaking charitable acts is that it helps them appreciate their own fortune more.[36] On this issue there needs to be a word of caution. It has long been recognised that being kind to others can kindle happiness in both benefactor and beneficiary, and recent psychology experiments confirm this truth.[37] Quoting such evidence, journalists and popular psychologists frequently urge us to give a stranger a compliment or volunteer at a homeless shelter. But doesn't this sort of advice seem rather empty? In offering simple dictates such advice fails to consider the underlying motivation required to make charitable acts effective. I might help out at a homeless shelter and feel nothing but resentment towards those who have used my free time. Indeed, the major reason many of us ignore suggestions to assist others is not because we lack the time or the resources – it is because we simply do not feel inclined to do so.

Morality will be touched on in chapter 7, so for now we shall put to one side the rights and wrongs of charitable acts. Instead we will focus on the reasons why we do, or do not, feel motivated to help others. The primary reason appears to involve empathy. Most of those we aid are close friends and members of our family. Because we know them well we are able to empathise with them to a far greater extent than with other people. When my friend is upset at having failed an exam I understand how dismayed she is because I know how hard she worked and what it meant to her. Empathising with her leads me to act compassionately and comfort her. Compare this with a stranger I pass in the street who is also upset. I feel some empathy for him because I know how it feels to be distressed, but this is severely limited by the fact that I have no idea why he feels so sad. If he explained his situation my sympathy would probably increase and I may feel compelled to help, but still my empathy for my friend would be much greater than for this man and my inclination to assist the two would reflect this.

Empathy provides the motivation to act compassionately. Without it we either lack the impulse to do anything or, if we do act, we can feel resentful and irritated. As such, the key to effective charitable action is to build empathy first, which will then create the desire to help. To advocate the development of empathy is not to say that complimenting a stranger or volunteering at a homeless shelter are terrible ideas. Doing these things may benefit all concerned, but the point is that if they are not done in the right frame of mind they may provide little emotional benefit to the benefactor. Building empathy for a person or group of people and then acting on the resulting compassion is far more likely to make you see the positive aspects of your assistance than blindly joining the first voluntary organisation you come across.[38]

Forgiving

Empathy can also assist happiness in another way. In the previous chapter we saw that feeling anger towards someone for a prolonged period of time can inhibit happiness by resulting in the build up of much negative emotion. By contrast, forgiving someone for a transgression can allow you to discard these emotions and feel better. Empathising with the offender is one way of doing so. By understanding why they acted as they did you may feel pity towards them more than anger.

It is important to note that forgiveness does not require you to excuse the injury or to re-establish a relationship with the transgressor. It is a letting go on your part of the anger and resentment you feel. If you find empathising difficult, recalling a time you committed an injury and were forgiven by someone else could help inspire you to forgive. If neither of these suggestions work, bear in mind that the longer you feel upset, the more harm you are doing yourself. What is the point in that? Nelson Mandela was once asked how he was able to forgive his jailers. He replied, 'When I walked out of the gate I knew that if I continued to hate these people I was still in prison.'[39]

Reducing rumination

One of the reasons sustained anger affects people so badly is because it encourages them to run over unhappy events repeatedly. In a similar manner, when we worry excessively about something our rumination tends to focus on possible negative consequences, which obviously inhibits happiness. As we noted in the last chapter, some reflection is beneficial because it helps us to make sense of past events and prepare for future ones, but several studies have found that too much rumination can reinforce rather than relieve feelings of anxiety, inadequacy and unhappiness.[40] What can be done to reduce harmful over-thinking? One of the most obvious solutions is to discuss the matter with someone else. Frequently, another person is able to provide objective judgement and allay your fears. An alternative plan is to engage in an engrossing activity whenever you start to feel yourself being lured into a bout of self-analysis. Complete distraction can allow your mind breathing space and if you come back to the problem you will likely do so with a clearer head. A third strategy is to block a fixed time in the future specifically for contemplation, which should be limited to a reasonably short period. Designating a particular time for rumination allows you to get on with things for the rest of the day and restricting that period keeps your thinking focused. Finally, ask yourself, 'Will I care about this when I'm lying on my deathbed?' Doing so can bring a sense of perspective to things that in the grand scheme are really pretty trivial and insignificant.[41]

Now a caveat: while obsessive thinkers may find the above advice useful in the short-term, it does not really address the heart of the problem. Talk to a friend and you may feel better about a particular issue, but there will always be another dilemma next week and another the week after. In order to move from merely coping with excessive rumination to averting it, we need to try and adopt a different way of thinking. Cognitive therapy, invented by Aaron Beck in the 1960s, provides a way of doing so.[42] It recommends people challenge their way of interpreting events and by doing so realise the irrationality of many of their beliefs. In effect, it prompts you to argue against yourself by asking you to seek evidence to back up your claims, consider alternative explanations and work out the realistic implications of different courses of action. Say, for example, that I cannot stop worrying about an upcoming job interview. Cognitive therapy would suggest that I first analyse the reasons for my concern. Do I really know nothing about hairdressing? I have been sculpting people's barnets for the last 4 years, so surely I must have picked up something. In fact, when I look over my experience I really know quite a lot. There are some areas I could learn more about, although I can read about these before the interview. But what if I do not get the job? Won't that make me a failure? No, it means the particular interviewer I met thought someone else was better suited to the role, but that is just one judgement and does not mean I lack any talent. The successful applicant may have been cutting hair for a lot longer than myself or have simply performed better on the day. Cognitive therapy encourages you to take action over the things you can affect and accept those you cannot. It also replaces the pessimistic habit of attributing permanent causes to bad events (e.g. I am ugly) with the more optimistic view that bad events have specific explanations (e.g. This particular person believes I am ugly, others find me attractive).

Cognitive therapy is not limited to dealing with concerns about specific events. Its approach can also be applied to more general worries, such as the fear of becoming a victim of crime or terrorism, which we will look at now to highlight how the technique can be used. High profile incidents reported in the media can distort our perception of the actual level of risk posed by these threats, so cognitive therapy would advocate trying to rationally assess the available evidence. One of the easiest places to start is to look at crime rates. On first inspection it would seem that over the course of the twentieth century there was a large rise in crime: in England and Wales the number of indictable offences per thousand population in 1900 was 2.4 and in 1997 the figure was 89.1.[43] Looking more closely, though, there are a number of problems with using these statistics to assess how concerned we should be about crime. Insurance companies only accept a claim if it is logged with the police, so the rise in domestic insurance since the 1930s partly explains the significant increase in reported crimes.[44] There was also growing pressure throughout the twentieth century for police to record crimes more accurately (especially to stop classifying items as lost rather than stolen if the case seemed unlikely to be solved).[45] Furthermore, comparing particular types of crimes across time periods is especially difficult because the categories used, and the sorts of misdemeanours that go in them, have changed over the years.

With so much uncertainty surrounding crime statistics it is probably best to try and focus on a more definite area. Homicide (murder, manslaughter and infanticide) is regarded as one of the more reliable police figures because it has a high report rate and is less likely to be misclassified. The threat of violent crime is also a more scary prospect than other offences. So, how many homicides were committed in England and Wales in 2012 (the latest available data)? 552 or 9.7 people per million population. Admittedly, this has risen from the 354 killed in 1967 (7.3 people per million population), but I still have a very slight 0.0001% chance of being unlawfully killed.[46] Even in the gun heavy USA I am more likely to croak it by tripping over than I am to die at the hands of a lunatic.[47] In fact, in both Britain and the USA a far greater risk is posed by driving a car.[48]

If the risk of being a homicide victim is low, the chances of dying in a terrorist attack are almost minute. Since the late 1960s (when the US State department started counting such things) the number of Americans who have died as a result of international terrorism, including the September 11th attacks, is roughly the same number as have been killed over the same period by lightening or accidents involving deer.[49] Cognitive therapy does not advocate ignoring risks: to do so would be reckless. When they are real – as they are, for instance, in the cases of smoking, obesity and alcoholism – it makes sense to be concerned about them in proportion to the dangers they actually pose. Ignoring regular alcohol over-indulgence, for example, may mean you are happier in the short term, yet ultimately it could significantly shorten your life. All cognitive therapy argues for is that we try to take a rational and considered approach when assessing the available evidence, as we have done with the risks posed by crime and terrorism. While over-thinkers will always be prone to some degree of excessive analysis, repeatedly **applying the techniques of cognitive therapy to specific and general worries can help develop an alternative way of thinking**, which over time may at least partially replace old thought processes. Doing so should also reduce the urge to over-analyse.

There is one final point worth mentioning before moving on. Barry Schwartz and his colleagues made an interesting observation when they distinguished between two decision-making styles used for making purchases.[50] In the first, a person searches for the best possible product available at the lowest price. They investigate the market thoroughly and even after they have bought a product they keep re-evaluating their decision. In the second, a person looks for a product that satisfies their needs and is not extortionately priced. When they find one that meets their criteria they buy it without exploring further and do not reappraise their decision. Those who buy according to the first style may get the best deal, but frequently they will not be as happy with their decision as those who used the second approach. No one takes the first or second strategy exclusively, but most people will veer towards one or the other on average. Those who adopt the first method may find that by using some of cognitive therapy's ideas they become happier not only with the products they decide to buy, but also with their decisions more generally.

Exercise

Cognitive therapy, with its belief that we can alter our attitudes using the power of thought alone, is in keeping with the central argument of this chapter, indeed of this whole book: we can become happier by changing our outlook rather than our life circumstances. There is, however, one area where a change in lifestyle can have a significant impact not only on happiness, but also on lifespan. Abundant research has found that regular physical activity a few times a week significantly reduces the risks of developing a broad range of diseases.[51] **Exercise has also been shown to relieve depression and increase happiness levels** (although these benefits may not be felt during the actual exercise!).[52] While the exact reasons for the health and mood benefits of physical activity are under debate, the huge scale of the evidence available should rouse more of us from the sofa. There are certainly obstacles hindering many people from engaging in regular exercise. Gyms can sometimes seem like over-sized hamster cages, sedentary jobs with long commutes and memories of being the last one picked to play can all be rather off-putting. With a little imagination, however, almost everyone should be able to find a way of introducing a bit more physical activity into their daily life. Do not join a sports team if you loathe competition, maybe do try cycling to work or climbing stairs rather than using lifts. The more exercise you get, the better it will be for your health but, as long as you do it regularly, anything that makes you warm and slightly out of breath will be beneficial.

Summary

The main advice of this chapter has been:

Slow adaptation to positive events by:
- Avoiding enjoying the same thing too often
- Altering the way you go about activities you must repeat frequently
- Finding more happiness inducing activities and varying them frequently

Savour everyday life by:

- Practising mindfulness
- Reminding yourself that each day could be your last
- Reminiscing about positive events from the past
- Undertaking charitable acts motivated by empathy

Let go of anger by:

- Empathising with the offender
- Remembering when someone else forgave you
- Acknowledging that holding on to anger hurts you

Reduce rumination by:

- Discussing your problems with someone
- Distracting yourself with an engrossing activity
- Blocking out a limited time specifically for contemplation
- Asking whether you will care about the issue on your deathbed
- Practising cognitive therapy

Take regular exercise because it can:

- Reduce the risk of a broad range of diseases
- Relieve depression and increase happiness

This chapter has outlined some initial advice for increasing happiness. While the general nature of these suggestions can be used in every aspect of life, the next chapter looks at happiness in a more specific area – work.

4
Work

How do you feel when you read the title of this chapter? Do cheerful and positive images spring to mind or does the very mention of the word make you reel in revulsion? If you fall into the latter category and Sunday nights are spent wishing Monday will never come, you are not alone. But it does not have to be this way! Much research has been performed on what makes people happy at work and it would be a great shame not to take advantage of it. From developing engaging challenges to reducing stress, this chapter will explain how to start enjoying your job.

Theory

When psychologists study happiness in the workplace (job satisfaction) they tend to make a distinction between a person's job environment (e.g. the level of skill required, the degree of personal control available, the variety of tasks performed, wages and the quality of feedback) and their attitude to the job. Traditionally, it was assumed that a person's attitude to their job was largely determined by their job environment. More recently, however, several different studies which followed subjects for significant periods of time found that despite promotions, reorganisations and job changes, job satisfaction for most participants was remarkably stable.[53] Some people tended to like whatever they were doing, while others switched jobs several times and felt equally dissatisfied in all of them. This suggests that happiness at work is more a feature of how someone perceives their job than what they are actually doing.

It must be acknowledged that there are some objections to this argument. It is possible that certain individuals tend to choose jobs that will suit them well, whereas others do not. In addition, it would be difficult to argue that a person who hates stress and uncertainty would feel equally satisfied in a job they are not fully qualified for with ambiguous objectives than in a position with clear goals which they have the skills to achieve. Nevertheless, there is still a strong case that job perception has a significant impact on job satisfaction.

In interviews with twenty-eight hospital cleaners, for example, it was found that while some regarded their job as menial and disliked it, others saw themselves as crucial to the successful operation of the hospital and took great pride in their work.[54] Here are people doing exactly the same job but seeing their work in very different ways. Such contrasts have prompted some researchers to suggest a tripartite division of attitudes to work:

1. There are those who see their job as a necessary evil – they do it to pay the bills but it only serves this end.

2. Others are more focused on having a career – they evaluate their current job based on how well it furthers their career ambitions.

3. Then there are people who just really love what they do – they work primarily not for financial reward or career prospects but because they find their job inherently fulfilling.[55]

It must be admitted that some jobs are more likely to promote the third view than the first, but no job is beyond redemption. It is also true that most people's attitude to their job changes quite frequently; one day you love it, the next you cannot wait for 5pm. For the rest of this chapter we are going to look at ways of encouraging ourselves to adopt the former viewpoint more often.

Flow

In the 1960s the unpronounceable Mihaly Csikszentmihalyi began investigating an experience he termed 'flow'.[56] When in this state people are so totally absorbed in what they are doing that they lose track of time, feel a sense of effortless control over their actions and cease to be self-conscious. There may be no felt emotion during the experience but it is usually highly enjoyable in retrospect.[57] Mihaly did not invent this psychological state – you have probably found yourself 'in the zone' while playing sport, painting or doing some other leisure activity – but he was the first person to scientifically study its causes and effects. Interestingly, he found that the conditions necessary to induce this state are very prevalent in the workplace, which means that there is the potential to take the same pleasure in our jobs as we do in our favourite hobbies.

Flow can occur at any time but, through many experiments, Mihaly discovered that the following circumstances, when found together, are most likely to cause it:

- There is a challenge which requires skill
- You completely concentrate on what you are doing
- Your goals are clear
- Immediate feedback allows you to assess your performance

It is very important that your skill level is appropriate for the challenge. If you possess insufficient skill then the challenge appears insurmountable and you are likely to become anxious. If, however, the challenge is too easy, you will probably find it boring. Consider giving a client presentation. Turn up with insufficient knowledge of the product you are pitching and you are likely to feel overwhelmed. Conversely, if you are reeling off the same patter for the umpteenth time it will probably be a very boring experience. Come prepared to your first talk with adequate knowledge and bat some tough questions over the boundary before sealing the deal, however, and you will probably be elated. There is one proviso though; you should see the benefits of activities for their own sake rather than because of their consequences. In the presentation example, for instance, if you give a great performance it should not matter whether you are awarded the contract or not: what counts is that you wanted to do a really good job and you achieved that personal ambition.

Now, you might be thinking that this is fine for corporate high-flyers jetting off to high-level meetings, but what about the rest of us?

Although it must be admitted that some jobs are inherently more conducive to creating flow, anyone can achieve it at work. Mihaly provides the great example of a man working on a production line who had to perform the same task on each of the 600 units that passed in front of him each day. Instead of being dispirited by such repetition, he challenged himself to see how quickly on average he could complete his part of the assembly line process every shift. He approached his task as an Olympic athlete approaches their event: How can I break my record?[58] By being creative and setting your own goals instead of merely tackling the ones you are given, **it is possible to create flow in any job.** A caution, though, is that as your skills improve you run the risk of finding your original goals too easy and becoming bored with them, so be prepared to set new challenges when the time comes.

Stress

In an interesting experiment Mihaly found that most people reported experiencing flow more while doing their job than during their free time. Despite this, when asked whether they would rather be working or at leisure the preference was overwhelmingly for the latter.[59] Why should this be? One answer is that, despite the potential of work to be enjoyable, the emotional downsides that come with a job outweigh the benefits. For many people stress is foremost among these negatives. From the boss who demands too much to the difficulty of juggling professional and family commitments, excessive pressure can be a major problem of the workplace. If we can reduce the amount of stress we feel at work, though, we might go some way towards being able to better appreciate the positive aspects of the time we spend there. Stress is a highly individual response – some people can react calmly to something that would send others into a blind panic – and different circumstances call for very different solutions. As such, it would be hopeless to lay out specific rules for you to follow. Some general suggestions can be made, however, that might help you cope with, and minimise the occurrence of, stressful situations.

First, it is useful to understand what stress is. When you feel under excessive pressure your heart rate, blood pressure and breathing rate all increase while your senses become more alert. At the same time your sex drive, digestion and immune system are inhibited.[60] Your body responds in this way because, in the dangerous world primitive humans inhabited, you would have needed all the energy you could muster to escape a not very cuddly wooly mammoth. In the modern world such dangers are mercifully rare, but your body frequently over-reacts to the actual level of threat posed by a portly and balding member of middle management. One of the first ways to decrease stress levels, then, is to spot when we are over-reacting and realise the irrationality of the extent of our emotions. Cognitive therapy, discussed in the previous chapter, provides one method for doing so. It asks us to catch our negative thoughts and dispute the reasons we give for believing them. Even if they do have some limited basis, what is the realistic worst outcome? By probing distorted opinions we come to see the errors in our thinking.

If you have time, such disputation is usually best done through writing because the process of committing your thoughts to paper forces you to structure your thoughts in a way not possible inside your head. In a different way, discussing your problems with a confidante can also relieve stress. Apart from the fresh perspective another person can give, simply sharing your worries with a sympathetic listener can bring relief. Another tactic is to try meditating: lots of research indicates that meditation can relieve stress both immediately and over a sustained period.[61] Although the idea can seem quite alien if you have not tried it before, I strongly recommend it. Despite its use in a wide variety of religions it is perfectly possible to practice it in a non-religious manner. There are a large number of different types of meditation but most involve a conscious attempt to focus your attention in a non-analytical way. One of my favourites is simply to close my eyes and focus on my breathing. To help myself concentrate, as I breath in I say, 'breathing in I am breathing in', and as I breath out I say, 'breathing out I am breathing out'. During this time I try really hard not to think about anything else and centre all of my attention on my breathing.[62] After a few minutes of doing this I usually find that no matter how pent up I was before I started, I now feel much more peaceful and at ease. The cause of my troubles may not have gone away, but I am in a much better frame of mind to take a rational view of things.

In this section we have discussed a few ways of managing our emotional reactions to stress. After employing these techniques to gain a realistic picture of our situation we are then able to act on the factors we can influence (e.g. learning how to operate the company's new computer system). We should also be able to recognise the elements we cannot control (e.g. whether the company will go bankrupt). An important part of managing stress is identifying these uncontrollable factors and making a conscious decision not to brood on them. If your company has a realistic chance of going under then it would be sensible to make a contingency plan, but once you have done what you can, **worrying about something you cannot influence is a complete and utter waste of time.**

Social Status

Something many people also spend time agonising over is their salary, but are the fat cats taking home the biggest wages any happier than the rest of us? Yes, slightly.[63] Hang on one second, didn't chapter 2 say that in the western world additional wealth does not lead to extra happiness? Good spot, it did, but the rich are not happier on average because they have more money, they are happier because of the non-material benefits that wealth can bring; in particular, social status.[64] This is why, as mentioned earlier, despite great economic progress over the last fifty years in the economically developed countries, there has been almost no increase in average happiness levels.[65] Although a manual worker might earn a lot more than his father did for doing the same job, the social status accorded to their profession is still the same. It was the insight that it is relative, rather than absolute, wealth that affects happiness which led Henry Mencken to observe that a rich man is one who earns $100 more than his wife's sister's husband.[66] The importance of comparative wealth makes sense from an evolutionary perspective as well: higher social status corresponds to better matting opportunities. Therefore, our genes have a greater likelihood of survival if they encourage us to enjoy being further up the hierarchy.[67]

As a result of this inborn programming we are left with a choice: should we chase higher pay packets than our peers in order to reap the increase in happiness that higher social status brings, or rebel against our natural impulses and define our self-worth ourselves? As ever, the best option will be different for different people, but there are two reasons to prefer the latter. Firstly, there is by definition a finite amount of social status. Regardless of how affluent we all become, the proportion of people inhabiting the higher social rungs will remain the same. Secondly, relying on promotion and social advancement leaves us prey to the vicissitudes of fortune. No matter how heroically and fervently we might work towards winning the top job, chance can always stand in the way. When we refuse to rely on the approval of others to create a positive image of ourselves fate loses its power over us. Indeed, in one experiment it was found that those who engaged less in social comparison were happier than those who did it more often.[68]

How do we learn to stop using others as a yardstick? The instinct to measure ourselves against others is so strong that to renounce it completely would be both impossible and unwanted – some mild social comparison can be useful to inspire and motivate us. What we can do, however, is lessen the degree to which we do it. There are essentially two complimentary ways to achieve this. In the first, we focus on making a conscious effort to reduce the amount of social comparison we indulge in. The techniques outlined while discussing rumination are applicable here because they help to curb the tendency to obsess about social position and realise the futility of doing so. This sentiment was wonderfully captured by Percy Shelly in his poem *Ozymandias*. He tells us of a collapsed statue in the desert:

> And on the pedestal these words appear:
> 'My name is Ozymandias, king of kings:
> Look on my works, ye Mighty, and despair!'
> Nothing beside remains. Round the decay
> Of that colossal wreck, boundless and bare,
> The lone and level sands stretch far away.

In the second method, our efforts are channelled towards promoting a positive self-image that does not rely on what others think. Remember the hospital cleaners we discussed at the start of this chapter. Those who liked their job saw the hidden value they brought to the patients. Without being given any great recognition by others they took pride in what they did because they viewed maintaining a hygienic hospital as an inherently worthwhile task. **If you see value in what you do, it becomes important regardless of what others think.** Give thought to the fact, too, that all of your actions, however small, have an impact. Delivering the internal mail might seem like a mundane task, but dire consequences might ensue if certain letters were lost. Likewise, replacing the cartridge in the communal photocopier could lead to a chain of positive events that leads who knows where!

Martin Seligman, a renowned psychologist, also has some useful advice. He recommends that at work we focus on nurturing our best strengths, instead of endlessly worrying about improving skills that come less naturally.[69] You might be wonderful at analysing information but terrible at presenting. While it is probably a good idea to work on being able to deliver a reasonable presentation, you are not a terrible employee because you find it difficult. Everyone has different talents and rather than focus on becoming the next Martin Luther King you would do far better to tolerate your weaknesses and enjoy the satisfaction that using your strengths brings.

Summary

This chapter began with the assertion that job perception is more important for happiness at work than the actual job. As a consequence of this, it has been argued that individuals have the potential to make themselves happier at work. The main advice for doing so has been:

Create flow by engaging in tasks which meet the following conditions:
- There is a challenge which requires skill
- You completely concentrate on what you are doing
- Your goals are clear
- Immediate feedback allows you to assess your performance
- You see the benefits of activities for their own sake

Reduce stress by:
- Practising cognitive therapy
- Discussing your problems with someone
- Meditating

Engage in social comparison less by:
- Using the techniques designed to avoid excessive rumination (see chapter 3)
- Seeing value in what you do regardless of what others think
- Nurturing your strengths

There is one last piece of advice before we move on. Several years ago I was travelling in a car with a friend, worrying about which job I should apply for. 'Just pick the one that pays the most,' he said, 'you aren't meant to like work, it's just a way to make money so you can enjoy your free time.' The whole thrust of this chapter has been completely against such a belief, but he was right in one respect: we should not spend too much time agonising over what would be our perfect job. Yes, some people are wholly unsuited to their current position and would do well to seek a change. The vast majority, though, can probably find a lot more enjoyment in their present job than they currently do. It is impossible to eliminate all stress or generate flow every working hour, yet by implementing the techniques outlined in this chapter we may just be able to throw away the idea that work is an unwanted imposition to be avoided as much as possible. There will always be times when work gets you down, but adopting the attitude that it must invariably be a loathsome experience is both a self-fulfilling prophecy and a waste of great swaths of your life. Work is a necessity, so why not try to enjoy it?

5

Relationships

You may have noticed a rather large omission from the previous chapter: the importance of good relationships. Even the most detestable job can be tolerated if you like your colleagues and many find chatting with team-mates to be one of the highs of their working day. Beyond the workplace, few are those who do not enjoy the company of friends and family (at least most of the time!). Despite this evidence, some claim that it is not friends and lovers who make people happy but happy people who attract friends and lovers. While this is a thought-provoking point, research carried out in this area suggests that the link works both ways: happy people are more likely to marry and have many friends, but romance and companionship also make most people happier.[70] As such, this chapter will offer advice on improving relationships in the hope that this will lead to greater happiness. Of all the relationships we have, probably the most important for the vast majority of people is the one they have with a significant other. Bearing this in mind, our focus will be on how to maintain a successful long-term romantic relationship (although much of the advice is also applicable to other close relationships).

Evolutionary Impulses

As with many other factors affecting happiness, when discussing romantic relationships it is helpful to begin by exploring the evolutionary origins of our psychological mechanisms because a basic grasp of why we think the way we do can elucidate many problems. The most fundamental point to understand is that, from an evolutionary perspective, the sole purpose of your body is to provide a means for your genes to replicate themselves.[71] Evolution favoured mental and physical developments in humans which promoted this end most successfully. Consequently, our minds and bodies have evolved to encourage and facilitate the reproduction and survival of as many offspring as possible.

Because human society varies, long or short-term mating strategies will be optimum in different circumstances.[72] Consequently, both men and women are capable of adopting either approach. The practicalities of reproduction, though, mean that on balance women are more inclined to a long-term strategy, whereas a short-term plan is more efficient for men. It takes a woman a minimum of nine months to produce a child. In the same time, a man, provided he is more Mr Darcy than Mr Collins, can sire tens, if not hundreds, of mini-replicas. The much greater time investment made by women impels them to be more discerning when they choose a lover. Additionally, in primitive times a woman's progeny had a much greater chance of surviving to adulthood if its father supported them both. As a result, the primary characteristics women look for in potential husbands are commitment and resources.[73] Conversely, the minimal time investment required by men to reproduce meant that, despite the risk of many offspring dying in childhood, spreading their seed as far and wide as possible could result in more sons and daughters reaching reproductive age than pursuing an exclusively monogamous relationship.

The natural differences between the sexes are why, when an attractive man and woman randomly approached members of the opposite sex on a university campus and offered them a quick shag, 100% of the women gave an emphatic no and 75% of the men leapt at the opportunity.[74] Indeed, while most of the women propositioned were offended or insulted, many of the men who declined the offer were apologetic, citing previous commitments. Despite high male sexual appetite, however, the female preference for dedicated stable partners meant that solely pursuing a short-term mating strategy would have been detrimental to ancestral man's breeding prospects. Indeed, besides female pressure to settle down, there are many benefits to men of long-term mating including increasing the odds that they are the father of a particular child, reducing the risk of contracting a sexually transmitted disease and improving the likelihood of their offspring reaching adulthood. Men, therefore, are fully capable of engaging in a long-term mating strategy involving commitment and monogamy. Because of the ease with which they can reproduce, though, evolution has found it expedient to maintain their wandering eye. Conversely, under certain circumstances prehistoric women could have found benefits in short-term mating, such as securing attractive genes for her offspring, acquiring resources in exchange for sex and switching to a better long-term mate. Generally speaking, though, the most expedient mating strategy for primeval humans was more long-term for women and short-term for men. Although we inhabit a completely different world to the one in which our ancestors lived, their evolved psychology remains with us and it is important to keep this in mind when discussing relationships.

Lust

Nowhere is this evolutionary overhang more pervasive than in the realm of desire. Male sexual fantasies generally place emphasis on physical gratification, sometimes involving strangers or multiple partners. Female fantasies, by contrast, more usually involve a single intimate partner and focus on an emotional connection.[75] For most women, a sense of close contact and attachment are crucial to erotic encounters, whereas for men raw lust is the engine of seduction. It is this natural insatiable urge which causes a man walking with his stylish and attractive wife to instinctively glance at another woman simply because she is wearing a short skirt. The occasional stray gaze, though, is only the beginning of the problems our inherited attitudes to sex cause in the modern world.

In one study, groups of men were asked to rate the attractiveness of, and their commitment to, their current partners after being shown photographs of either very desirable or average-looking women. Compared to the men who were shown pictures of average-looking women, those who had seen the better-looking women not only judged their current partners to be less attractive, but were also found to be less committed to, and satisfied with, them.[76] Such findings must raise concern about the pernicious effects of airbrushed advertising and internet pornography. The tricks these illusions of femininity play on us, however, can be managed to some extent. Men need to make an effort to remind themselves that the mirages they see on bill boards should not be used to judge the women they meet in real life. Also, as difficult as it might be, many women would benefit from deliberately not comparing themselves with such images.

In this respect, it might be helpful to know that in a study which showed men and women a selection of nine female figures, when asked which body shape men preferred women consistently chose figures which were substantially slimmer than those the men in the study actually liked most.[77] The message from this is clear, from a male point of view thinner does not equal better looking. Besides which, there is a great deal more to attraction than physical appeal. It may be true that men are frequently drawn towards someone initially because of their looks, but even the shallowest person knows that there is a lot more to desire than mere appearance. The best looking woman at the party may seem irresistible from the other side of the room, but spend five minutes in her company and you might prefer to throttle yourself than date her. The reverse is also true when you meet someone with a stunning personality. Attraction is a complicated affair and we grossly misrepresent it when we place too much emphasis on the power of appearance alone. If both sexes make a conscious effort to keep in touch with reality, the damaging psychological effects of fictitious images might, if they cannot be eliminated, at least be diminished.

Conflict

While sexual attraction may be a potential source of marital conflict, it is only one among many. Interestingly, the most prominent marriage researcher, John Gottman, believes that what differentiates couples who stay together from those who separate is not whether they argue (everyone does) but *how* they argue.[78] He reached this conclusion after studying hundreds of couples in a purpose-built research apartment and highlights four features of the way partners destined to split argue:

1. General criticisms are made instead of specific complaints
2. Contempt is shown

3. Defensive statements are made instead of apologies
4. One person completely disengages from the argument

Before you become alarmed that you recognise a few of these symptoms in your own relationship, Gottman explains that all couples display one or all of these elements in some of their arguments. If they feature heavily in almost every discussion, however, there is a problem. Whether they appear frequently in your arguments or not, understanding why they occur and how to prevent them is beneficial to all.

Perhaps not surprisingly, men and women tend to encourage different aspects of bad arguments. Speaking very generally, when compared to women, men are:

- Less willing to express/talk about emotion
- Likely to overreact at an earlier stage of an argument
- Inclined to a rosier view of the state of their marriage

By contrast, women:

- Are more willing to express/talk about emotion
- Experience a wider range of emotions and more intense emotions
- Display greater empathy[79]

These characteristics mean that women, on average, are more willing to enter into difficult emotive discussions than their partners. Because men are susceptible to overreact, they frequently protect themselves from being emotionally overwhelmed by disengaging from an argument. Distressed by her husband's apparent refusal to acknowledge her views, in an attempt to make him participate in the discussion, a woman is now more likely to turn her initial specific complaint ('you did not wash the dishes') into a general criticism ('you are always so lazy').[80] Hijacked by their emotions, both sides are now likely to show contempt for each other and make defensive statements instead of apologies.

Marital researchers offer a variety of ways to prevent and deal with such situations. For men, the advice is not to avoid conflict. When your wife brings up a grievance it is frequently because of her concern to maintain a healthy relationship. Much more than solutions, which are often seen by her as attempts to dismiss her complaints as inconsequential, what matters most to her is that you acknowledge and understand her feelings. For women, the main recommendation is to be sensitive to the fact that men are more prone to being emotionally overwhelmed. As such, complaints should be kept specific and expressed in a non-confrontational manner.[81]

Both parties are advised to try and remain as calm as possible. Once passions are roused it is almost impossible to hear clearly and speak reasonably. Recommend a break if emotions start to run wild and focus on something else during it; by doing so you are far more likely to see things in perspective. Also crucially important for women and men is empathy. While it may come more naturally to women, it is very important that both people in an argument try to understand each other's point of view. Doing so allows the real issues to be addressed. Lastly, perhaps the best thing either advocate can do is make attempts to repair the rift. John Gottman has found that even couples whose quarrels regularly feature the four elements of bad arguments stand a chance of staying together if they are good at making up.[82] It takes mutual co-operation, though, for this to work: it is not enough simply to offer your hand, you must also be ready to accept your partner's.

Lasting Love

Moving away from managing conflict, suppose you meet someone who you are confident you will be attracted to for a long time. You have the occasional argument but you always make up afterwards. What is the likelihood that marrying this person will make you lastingly happier? The results of a huge German study spanning fifteen years suggest that your chances vary.[83] The investigation found that, on average, as people move towards marriage they usually experience a lift in happiness, but that after the big day this gradually declines until, after approximately two years, it has worn off and they return to whatever baseline of happiness they were at before getting hitched. Despite this rather depressing conclusion, there is hope. While the researchers found two years to be the average length of the marriage happiness boost, there was significant variation amongst the couples they surveyed. Some reported a sustained increase in happiness that lasted well beyond two years and remained throughout the study, while others were actually less happy after two years of marriage than they were before. What, then, separates successful couples from the rest?

The most basic point is really blindingly obvious; have a reasonable number of common interests and opinions. There will always be some things about which even the most well matched partners permanently disagree. There is no solution to these debates except to respect and tolerate each other's views. Compromise may also be essential if two goals are incompatible. There is a limit, however, to even the most flexible people. As such, while it is wise to check before you wed that you have compatible ambitions and viewpoints, it is essential that throughout married life you find and develop shared passions. Making the effort to do so prevents you gradually drifting apart until you find yourselves living separate lives under the same roof.

Indeed, it is effort which lies at the heart of thriving marriages. Only by remembering not to take your partner for granted and consciously fighting adaptation can you both sustain the hedonic benefits of marriage. It is natural to be appreciative the first few times your partner irons your shirts, but after several years it is all too easy to forget how generous they are and, instead of thanking them for their work, only rebuke them when they forget to do their 'job'. Likewise, after a few years there is the potential to assume you know everything about your spouse and become bored by their conversation. But happy couples talk – a lot. They take an active interest in what one another has been doing and regularly express admiration and gratitude. Each partner is also conscious of how their actions and inactions might affect the feelings of the other.[84]

In essence, successful couples make the effort to sustain the enthusiasm for, and interest in, each other that they experienced when they first fell in love. It is undoubtedly impossible to retain the feeling of being hopelessly besotted with someone that accompanies the first flushes of love, but by preserving as many of the habits which developed during that time it is possible to build a wonderful, caring, affectionate and enduring friendship. Lasting love does not fall by chance on some: it comes to those who commit to nurturing it.

Summary

The main findings of this chapter are:

In general evolution has favoured the development of:
- A short-term mating strategy in men
- A long-term mating strategy in women

To prevent this causing conflict:
- Women should be less concerned when their partner finds other women sexually attractive
- Men should give their partner the attention they deserve

Bad arguments can be prevented and dealt with if:
- Men acknowledge and understand their partner's feelings
- Women express complaints in a non-confrontational manner and keep them specific
- Both try to remain calm during discussions and take a break if needed
- Both try to empathise with each other
- Both make attempts to repair the rift

Marriage stands a greater chance of working if couples:
- Compromise a reasonable amount
- Find and develop shared interests
- Remember not to take each other for granted
- Communicate admiration and gratitude to each other regularly

6

Finding Meaning

Having considered the various ways of feeling happier it is now time to look at the third type of happiness, that which concerns finding meaning in life. Joy and contentment may come to a person in abundance, but in a more sombre moment of reflection they might ask, 'What's the point of all this? Why, when all is said and done, does it matter that I exist?' By asking such questions we recognise that there is more to life than happiness types one and two – that even if we have attained each of them in plenty there is still something missing. That something is a meaning in life, a sense that there is a point or purpose to your existence.

To some, the idea that life might have a meaning is ridiculous. How can the life of a single person whose creation was the result of evolutionary luck and who is living on just one of the billions of planets in the universe have any objective purpose? The religious believer may be able to find an answer, but the agnostic or atheist may be hard pressed to come up with a reply. Faced with such bleakness it is easy to fall into a well of despair where life is seen as futile and worthless. But does life need to have an objective purpose in order to be meaningful? When I say, 'My mum means a lot to me,' I am not implying that she fulfils any purpose for me, but instead suggesting that I value her in some way. In a similar vein, to ask, 'What is the meaning of life?' can be interpreted as enquiring what we value in life. By holding certain things to be important we give our own meaning to life. The question then becomes, how do we decide what is worth valuing? Again, those with religious conviction can look to their faith to instruct them, but what of the non-believer, where should they turn for guidance?

Philosophy, it will be argued, holds the key. Unfortunately in the West it is frequently seen as a highly intellectual enterprise suitable only for those with a mega-brain, who if they were not picking Kant to pieces would be studying nuclear physics. In part this reputation has developed because much modern philosophy uses a barrage of technical terms which bamboozle the reader and discussion is frequently more about interpreting what different philosophers have said rather than working through the central issues which philosophy raises. It is true that academic philosophy has its place and studying what other thinkers have said can stimulate new ideas, but asking basic questions about ourselves and the world we live in is one of the most natural activities and consequently philosophy should not be regarded as inaccessible and exclusive. With a little effort anyone is capable of philosophising, they just need to focus on the problems of philosophy rather than get lost in discussions about the correct interpretation of Wittgenstein.

In what follows, this book will attempt to show how philosophy can be used to provide a guide to what is worth valuing, and hence what may give life meaning. To ease understanding a minimum of technical language will be used and there will be little reference to the opinions of different thinkers. Despite this, some passages may seem a bit slow, but this is necessary in order to be sure the argument put forward is clear and rigorous. It is also important to note that what is said should only be taken as an indication of one possible argument. Readers wishing to think more deeply about the issues tackled are advised to consult the further reading at the end of the book.

Before we begin, however, it is worth explaining why philosophy is the best tool for finding a meaning to life. It is because philosophy (as practised in the West) uses reason as the basis of all argument. Meditation, revelation, intuition and other forms of non-rational enquiry can all be used to investigate basic beliefs, but frequently the results are very difficult to describe in words, inconsistent and impossible for anyone other than the person having the experience to verify. Rational enquiry, by contrast, can be accurately described, has accepted standards and can be tested by anyone. As we shall see later, humans do make mistakes when using reason, but what is important is that these can be recognised and addressed by other people. Although reason may not be infallible, it is the best tool we possess for understanding the world and its power is regularly exposed by some of the most inquisitive people in the world – children.

Why?

Many adults have experienced the frustration of a child who poses a seemingly innocent question and then proceeds to ask 'Why?' to every answer. Although the experience can be a draining one, the method that children use is not only highly rational, it also exposes a central problem we face when trying to determine what is worth valuing: the difficulty of finding a base of knowledge on which to justify valuing anything. Consider the following breakfast table encounter:

Q: Why do you go to work?
A: So I can earn money in order to pay our bills and buy you food.
Q: But you work very hard. Why don't you work less?
A: Because then I would have less money to buy you nice things like presents.
Q: Why is it important to have nice things?
A: Because nice things are enjoyable.
Q: Why is enjoying ourselves important?
A: Well I suppose enjoyment is part of what makes life worth living.
Q: But why is that true?

After a succession of answers and whys the final answer is usually an exasperated, 'Because I say so!' But this response only reflects a lack of patience or knowledge. If we possessed limitless tolerance and a thorough understanding of the subject area being probed, there are three possible outcomes to the conversation:

1. The series of answers and whys is infinitely long.

2. The initial statement is used as the answer to one of the later whys so that the series of questions and justifications forms a loop.

3. The series of answers and whys terminates with certain statements being self-justifying.

It is clear that if we are to discover what is worth valuing then outcomes 1 and 2 will be of no use. 1 provides no base on which to justify anything and 2 only takes us back to our original statement. Outcome 3, however, does provide a foundation which can enable us to build up support for holding particular values. In order to assess what values can be supported, therefore, we first need to understand what can make a statement self-justifying and which statements meet this requirement.

Certainty

By definition, a self-justifying statement is one that requires no further justification. It is a statement of which we can be absolutely certain because it cannot be questioned. But is there anything of which an individual can be completely certain? Consider the following scenario.

A week ago Michelle lent her friend Hillary her favourite red satin shoes. Hillary now tells Michelle that she wore them to a ball and, unfortunately, her clumsy husband Bill spilt red wine on them and they were ruined so she has thrown them out. Because they are friends Michelle believes her, and that belief is reinforced when George, Donald and other people at the party corroborate Hillary's story. A few days later, however, Michelle bumps into Hillary in a restaurant and notices that she's wearing some spotlessly clean red satin shoes. Next time they meet, Michelle confronts Hillary and asks if she still has her shoes. She denies it, but Michelle insists on scouring her wardrobe. Sure enough, right at the back are some red shoes. Hillary, however, claims she has always owned them and that they are different from the pair she borrowed. They look so similar to the original shoes that Michelle feels confident Hillary is lying, but the longer Hillary insists they are different the more Michelle questions her memory.

What exactly were the shoes like? The more Michelle tries to imagine them, the harder it becomes to remember their precise shape. Confused but suspicious, she returns home where she comes across a photo of herself wearing the shoes. Surely this will settle the matter! Michelle storms back to Hillary's house and demands to compare the photo to the shoes. At first they look identical, but as Hillary opens the curtains and the room becomes brighter Michelle cannot be quite so sure. In fact, as she turns the shoes in the light they seem to subtly change colour, looking identical to the photo one moment and different the next. Is Hillary a thief or is Michelle paranoid?

We can only hope that, regardless of the truth, Hillary will give Michelle the shoes to make up for the fact that she ruined hers and they can both get on with more important business. The scenario does, however, raise a number of significant points concerning how much trust we can place in our sources of knowledge. First there is the testimony of others: despite assurance from several different people, Michelle cannot be sure that Hillary is telling the truth. Her memory is also susceptible to error and even her sense of perception can confuse her. If the colour of the shoes changes as they are exposed to differing amounts of light, what shall we call their true colour? For practical purposes we can describe them generally as red, but as soon as we try to be more precise we find that we cannot be absolutely certain of one specific colour.

'Ok,' you might say, 'I accept that I cannot be completely certain of what other people tell me, of my memory all of the time or of my sense of perception in certain circumstances, but I can be sure that I have lived for a certain period of time, that the world exists and that it is inhabited by other people like me.' Of even these most basic beliefs, however, we cannot be totally sure. As absurd as it may seem, it is possible that the world sprang into existence five minutes ago with all of your memories intact. It is also possible that what you perceive to be the world is really an illusion generated by a virtual reality machine your head is plugged into, in which case the other people you see may not be real either. In fact, the only thing of which you can be certain is that there are thoughts which appear to be inside your head.[85] While it may be a relief to find that there is at least some certain knowledge, it is not much use by itself because without any other certain knowledge we cannot deduce anything else.

What to Believe?

Perhaps I can only know one thing with certainty, but on a day-to-day basis I feel confident that what I see before me really does exist and that my memory gives a reasonably accurate record of my life. I believe in these things because so many separate pieces of evidence seem to confirm them. When there is a biscuit in front of me, for example, the fact that I can not only see it but also touch, smell, taste and hear it break all convince me that what I am perceiving really is there. Likewise, although it is possible that all of my memories could have been artificially implanted into my brain five minutes ago, the testimony of others, physical evidence such as photographs and the vividness of my memories all persuade me that most of what I remember really did happen.

When evidence fits together consistently and is mutually explanatory it coheres. As a result, it increases the probability that a given explanation is correct. The downfall of philosophies which suggest that you are the only person who exists or that other people are products of a virtual reality machine is that while they are possible, the available evidence suggests that they are highly improbable. When deciding on what to value we need to accept that although we cannot be certain, evidence which coheres makes some beliefs more probable than others.

Faulty Reasoning

Before we can assess which things are more likely to be worth valuing, however, there are a number of stumbling blocks to overcome. Although reason is the best tool we have for understanding the world, we must be wary of our fallibility when applying it. Imagine that a coin has been tossed 20 times and every time it has landed on heads. Assuming the coin is not biased, would you bet on it being heads or tails next time it is thrown? After such a long run of heads, most people (myself included) feel that tails is more likely, but probability theory tells us that the odds of it being heads or tails are even.[86] This error of judgement is called 'the gambler's fallacy' and occurs because the brain has difficulty calculating probabilities quickly. This is just like an optical illusion – stare at it long enough and you can work out what is going on, but initially your brain is confused.

Other problems humans face when judging probabilities are that we can be overly influenced by the way information is presented and have difficulty in assigning reasonable estimates to real life problems that are hard to quantify. It is not only with probabilities that we encounter complications when applying reason: amongst other things, we are persuaded by communal opinion, biased to our current beliefs when appraising new evidence and see patterns where there are none. These quirks can lead to mistakes when trying to think through problems. Highlighting them does not suggest that we need to abandon rational thought, just that we should take care when we see an apparently obvious solution. Being aware of our ability to err is half of the battle won because recognising the causes of faulty thought helps us to be wary of them.

What Should We Value?

So far we have seen that we can never be certain of what is worth valuing but, while being vigilant against faulty reasoning, evidence which coheres will be more probable than anything else. As such, in order to decide what to value we need to determine which evidence coheres best. This is something that each individual should do for themselves but to help explain how this might be done I will outline what I believe is worth valuing and why.

As soon as I begin to look for evidence which coheres, however, I realise that there are a number of very important issues on which I simply cannot decide. What happens after we die, whether there is a god/s and, most fundamentally, why there is something rather than nothing are all questions for which no one answer seems more probable than any other. While instinct may usher me towards particular opinions, a rational look at the available evidence tells me that it is impossible to decide. This is perhaps rather disappointing, but do we need to know the answers to these questions in order to find value in life? I think not.

The world we have been thrown into is so full of wonder and beauty that it seems a privilege to be able to experience it. All of the evidence I see suggests that it is the experience of life which should be valued above all else. When I look at thousands of stars on a cloudless night or hear Jeff Buckley sing *Hallelujah* I cannot help but be overawed by the beauty of what is present. Such experiences are rare for many people, yet they do not need to be. I am currently in a flat in Manchester sitting at a small wooden table, but this table is capable of eliciting the most incredible wonder: the ebb and flow of the grain carries my attention across the surface and as I focus more intently on a particular knot or certain piece of joinery I wonder who built this table? Where did the trees grow from which it is made? Who planted them? How many birds nested in their branches? Where are those birds now? That such a mundane object can spark so much interest is incredible. Yet everything around us is full of curiosity and worthy of attention. The practicalities of surviving necessarily mean we have to ignore such fascination for large parts of each day, but it is during moments of wonder that we are able to glimpse the miracle of existence. From this perspective, experience should be what we value most and appreciating it is what gives life meaning.

To put this another way, imagine for a moment that for the rest of your life you are inexplicably placed inside a virtual reality machine from which you cannot escape. The world of the machine is enormous and incredibly rich in variety, with food and drink provided when you complete certain tasks. Besides undertaking sufficient jobs to ensure your survival, how would you spend your time? It would be natural to devote considerable effort to figuring out a way to escape, or at least discovering why you had been placed inside the machine. Suppose that you eventually conclude both of these efforts are futile, what then? It is my belief that under such circumstances the most satisfying way to live would be to marvel at the ingenuity of the world in which you found yourself – to investigate, enjoy and wonder at the experience. Faced with the uncertainty of lacking any knowledge about the reasons for ones existence, just as we are, you have to choose what to value – and experience, being the most incredible and fundamental part of existence, seems the best candidate.

Summary

The main points discussed in this chapter have been:
- Meaning in life is created by valuing certain things
- Justifications are needed when deciding what to value
- As nothing can be known for certain no justifications can be certain

- However, evidence which coheres suggests some opinions are more probable than others
- In my experience, evidence coheres to suggest that the experience of life is worth valuing and appreciating it is what gives life meaning

7

Exploring Meaning

The previous chapter looked at how to find meaning in life and it concluded with my own opinion – we should appreciate the value of experience. In order to explore what this means and how evidence coheres to suggest it, this chapter will address a series of questions that could be posed by a well-informed critic. Such an exercise will necessarily put forward a case for my personal views, but it can also be used by readers to see the ways in which they might critically assess their own opinions. Investigating opinions in this manner can reveal the key assumptions made as well as expose areas of weakness in an argument. After these areas have been uncovered we are in a better position to assess whether our thoughts should be modified.

(Q1) What do you mean when you say that appreciating experience gives life meaning?

In one respect, to appreciate something is to enjoy it. As such, I believe we should seek to enjoy the experience of living as much as possible. For some this will mean the exhilaration of a sky-dive, while for others it might be the wonder felt when contemplating the complexity of the human brain. In another sense, however, appreciation involves being grateful. In this respect appreciation implies that we should see life as a gift for which we should be thankful. Thanks for life is regularly expressed in most religions through different rituals, but if you do not know to whom or what you should be grateful, I suggest the best way to convey your gratitude is to regularly remember the contingency of your existence – to be aware that all experiences are temporary and should be enjoyed in the moment they are available.

So, appreciation means enjoying the experience of living and at the same time not taking that experience for granted. When you are actively aware of enjoying experience you recognise its value and by doing so make it meaningful. It is crucial to note the importance of conscious recognition in creating meaning. If someone were to go through life enjoying experience yet always taking it for granted, I think we would be justified in finding their life less meaningful than another person who enjoyed the same events but who also acknowledged their thankfulness for them. Without recognition of value, value cannot exist. Neither therefore, can there be meaning.

In emphasising the importance of enjoyment there is a danger of appearing to endorse a life centred solely around the pursuit of pleasure. There are, however, almost endless ways in which the world can be enjoyed. Delighting at the taste of a fresh mango is one, taking satisfaction in helping a drug addict rehabilitate themselves is another. Whether one form of enjoyment is better than another is addressed in Q7 but what I hope to have shown is that whichever form of enjoyment you choose, consciously appreciating it can give your life meaning.

(Q2) You assume the world is beautiful and a wonderful place to inhabit, but aren't you ignoring the presence of much misery, distress and ugliness?

First let us be clear about the meaning of the word 'beautiful'. I use it in a broad sense to suggest that the world is capable of providing much positive enjoyment. This will be different for different people and, as such, what is perceived as beautiful will vary from one individual to the next (for more on this issue see Q7). Despite this, however, there are many things in the world that most humans tend to find terrible, such as starvation, poverty and torture. Far from making me doubt the merit of valuing the wonder and beauty of experience, though, such negatives reinforce my belief in the value of appreciating positive experiences. It is appalling when awful events such as famines and wars occur, but we find them so distressing precisely because they are the opposite of what we desire. In such a way, the repulsion of misery, distress and ugliness point us towards what we should value. To use a food analogy; if I adore high quality chocolate, tasting a revolting chocolate substitute does not make me value high quality chocolate any less, it makes me appreciate the better product even more.

(Q3) *After a fantastic experience, why continue to live even though nothing may be that enjoyable again?*

The question fundamentally misunderstands the nature of appreciating experience. It is not a goal which can be reached, but an ongoing never-ending activity. Because the world can be enjoyed in so many ways there is always a different manner in which it can be appreciated. Suppose you played football from a very young age and when you grew up you won the World Cup. The joy and satisfaction at having reached a life-long goal which is very rare to achieve would be immense, and this would probably be the greatest emotional high you would ever experience. But what about the fulfilment of starting a football academy or the wonder of studying the night sky? The possibilities for enjoyment are limitless, so success in one area need not lead to the conclusion that there is no point continuing to exist.

(Q4) *Is it justifiable to use drugs to enhance experience?*

In answering this question it is important to differentiate between three different types of drug use. Firstly, there is recreational drug use involving the consumption of such things as ecstasy, cocaine and alcohol to generate a temporary emotional boost. Ignoring the legality of taking different substances, the main question to be answered when considering using them in this manner is whether the negative consequences (both potential and actual) are worth the positive ones? As all recreational drugs have at least some damaging side-effects, and many carry very serious risks, the balance of positive versus negative experiences would suggest mild use of some might be justifiable, but long-term over-use of any would be very inadvisable.

Drugs taken to alleviate a medical condition, such as pain-killers and anti-depressants, form the second type of drug use. Here the focus is on reducing and alleviating negative experiences rather than promoting positive ones and few would dispute the use of drugs in such circumstances. What some people do question is the third type of drug use, where substances are used to create an artificial emotional high over a sustained period of time, such as the drug soma in *Brave New World*. Apart from the possible harmful side-effects to ones physical health of using drugs in such a manner, there are several reasons to find it undesirable. Lacking the benefits of negative emotions outlined in chapter 2, it is possible to misjudge many situations and find yourself materially worse off. In addition, without any effort required to feel good it becomes very difficult to ever experience a sense of achievement. Finally, if you remain on an emotional high all of the time it becomes impossible to differentiate good from bad experiences. You adapt to your new emotional state and as a result happiness ceases to carry any meaning. Every day becomes a monotonous succession of boring happenings with no light or shade. Despite the initial potential appeal of inducing a permanent emotional high, seriously contemplating such a life makes one realise how very undesirable it would really be.

(Q5) You cite experience as your reason for valuing life, but what about the value of other things, such as love or morality?

Love and moral behaviour are worth valuing, but only because they help contribute to a more positive appreciation of experience. When love is reciprocated it is a positive experience for both people, but when love is damaging, such as in an abusive relationship, it losses its value because it ceases to contribute positively to experience.

(Q6) Why are you unable to decide on what happens after we die, whether there is a god/s and why there is something rather than nothing?

These issues are of fundamental importance and how a person answers them will have a considerable impact on what they value in life. With such a high impact, I believe any answer to each question should have much support. Any solution presented, however, always seems to contain many flaws. Take the idea that there is life after death, for example. All claims supporting such a theory rest on the assumption that there is some part of me which is non-physical and eternal. Modern science, though, seems to suggest that I am nothing but a collection of atoms. Clearly this presents a substantial hurdle to any claims of life beyond the grave.

But let us look to support the opposite hypothesis that there is no such thing as life after death. Proponents of this theory frequently claim that consciousness is nothing more than a by-product of the way the brain operates and when it ceases to function any sense of 'I' disappears with it. Apart from the fact that neurology is very far from being able to connect mental states to precise physical processes, there is also the abundant evidence of ghosts and spiritualists to explain. Whilst we cannot ever reach a certain conclusion on this issue, it seems reckless to decide one way or the other without one answer being considerably more probable than the alternative.

The same can be said for the existence of a god/s. It makes sense that there could be some being which created the universe, but with so many religions putting forward very different ideas of what that being may be like, it seems impossible to decide between them. Indeed, when we explore the issue of why there is something rather than nothing it becomes even harder to determine whether there is a god or not. Could the initial cause of the universe just be a blob of energy? Indeed, does there necessarily need to be an initial cause of the universe? Faced with so much uncertainty it seems impossible to decide.

These issues are central to how many people perceive the world, but I would caution readers against taking too firm a stance on any of them. In the preceding chapter we briefly looked at the ways in which the human brain can misinterpret evidence. Critics of religion frequently claim that believers fall into these traps when they attribute worldly events to divine intervention, but we can also overestimate what scientists can explain. Inexplicable events such as sightings of UFOs or ghosts are often written off as hoaxes. Many are, but when we genuinely cannot explain why an event has occurred, there is a tendency to believe scientists could account for the event if they had enough time and resources to devote to it. Such faith is misplaced. While scientists can provide reliable theories to describe how a huge amount of the world works, there is still a tremendous amount that is unknown. It is right to believe scientific theories when there is much evidence to support them, but to assume that scientists can explain everything, or will be able to in the future, makes everything appear definite, finite, obvious and unjustly robs the world of much of its mystery and fascination. Retaining an open mind not only keeps alive our sense of wonder; it also prevents us from falling prey to the tyranny of dogma.

(Q7) How can we know which parts of experience are more or less worth appreciating?

Appreciation is a subjective exercise. One person may take great satisfaction in solving crosswords, another might find them utterly dull. But although different individuals can have different tastes, we tend to think of some experiences as more worthwhile than others. Most people, for instance, would probably regard the fulfilment of composing a lengthy piece of music as better than the pleasure of eating strawberries and cream. The reasons for this are that writing music requires effort, time, commitment and the sacrifice of other pleasures, all of which simply eating does not. We are inclined to rank experiences which require endeavour as higher than those which do not. Despite widespread admiration for striving, though, we must remember that this is still a subjective preference – nothing makes the composer's labour objectively better than the strawberry eater's.

Stressing the subjective nature of appreciation is not to encourage the pursuit of easy pleasures, it merely highlights the importance of choosing what to value yourself rather than relying on other people's judgements. It also reminds us that it is possible to admire different elements of experience in different ways. Going on holiday, for instance, is quite often the source of much enjoyment, but in another way so can everyday life. To only ever appreciate the big moments and ignore the more subtle joys of your daily routine is to miss out on a fantastic opportunity.

What, though, of negative experiences? Is there anything to be appreciated in these? By themselves, there would appear to be nothing of value in them, but when used as a contrast to better experiences they serve a very important function. Without living through bad events you would have nothing to compare good events with. Indeed, unless you experienced them you would be incapable of fully enjoying better times.

Finally, we might ask how we are to decide between two experiences of apparently equal worth, such as being an ideal parent or a great explorer? We cannot. All we can do is take a best guess at which will most suit our situation, abilities and the needs of others. We must also accept that in choosing one we necessarily forgo the other.

(Q8) If the worth of different experiences is subjective, does this mean anything goes? For instance, if someone derived great enjoyment from killing would it be alright for them to commit murder?

Such a person is probably guilty of faulty reasoning or incoherent beliefs. Their idea that killing would be enjoyable is likely to be based on a false understanding of what they find enjoyable. If they insisted after much thought that they would still enjoy killing then we might ask if their beliefs were coherent. For example, would the pleasure of killing be worth the subsequent feeling of guilt, time spent in prison, ostracism by friends, etc? If they still held that killing would be the best option for them, we could not rationally argue against them any longer. Does this legitimise murder? It provides a case for how someone may rationalise murder, but it does not mean that we have to stand by and let them do as they please. Tolerance of another's beliefs is a positive thing. When someone else's actions put us in danger, however, we are justified in stopping them (see Q11 for a discussion of how to weigh up your interests versus those of others).

(Q9) You address the case of an individual who poses a threat to others, but what arguments could be used if the majority of a society believed they could attain better experiences by exploiting a minority of the population?

Such situations arose throughout the twentieth century and continue to occur in the twenty-first. Without appealing to objective moral standards it is difficult to argue against positions like this. It can be done though. Ultimately, what stops most of us from taking advantage of others is not the law or social convention, but empathy. Humans have an inbuilt ability to understand and share the feelings of others, which when exercised leads to compassion. Certainly some people are naturally more prone to empathy than others and physical as well as emotional distance affects how strongly it is felt. Almost everyone has the capacity for it, however, and it is empathy which lies at the heart of morality.[87] Developing and maintaining this ability not only benefits society, it also rewards individuals who practice it. People with a strong sense of empathy understand others better and, as a consequence, enjoy better relationships.

(Q10) Why do you believe empathy is central to morality?

When we read about a terrible event in the news, such as the disappearance of a young child, there are several reasons we may feel moral outrage. We might be upset that the law has been broken, fear that the same could happen to our own children, be perturbed at the abductor's apparent lack of conscience or lament the decay of social values. Above all else, though, I believe it is our empathy with both the victim and their parents that has the greatest effect on us. Imagining how scared the child must have been and recognising how distressing it would be as a parent in that situation are the main reasons we feel a moral wrong has been committed. Of course, there are many occasions when people act morally without feeling the slightest inkling of empathy. They might act out of habit, in order to comply with social convention or because of a whole host of other reasons. Despite this, if we were to assess why these reasons to act morally developed, we would find empathy as the root cause. Indeed, the most widely known moral instruction in the world, the golden rule, relies on empathy for it to function.[88] 'Do unto others as you would be done by' asks you to put yourself in the place of others. Without the ability to empathise this would be impossible.

(Q11) Do you endorse the golden rule?

As a general guide to moral action it serves as an excellent pointer. By asking us to consider the concerns of others and requiring that we envisage ourselves in their place it captures the essence of morality. There are some serious difficulties faced when applying the golden rule, however. Insufficient knowledge of another's situation can lead to problems when trying to imagine how they will interpret a particular action. You might, for example, see a frail old lady about to cross the road. Thinking that you would like to be helped in a similar situation, you take her by the arm and lead her to the other side. Most of the time it would be a reasonable assumption that the old lady would like some assistance. It is possible, though, that the lady has just returned from hospital and although she is weak she sees crossing the road as a test of her fitness. Doing it by herself could raise her confidence and self-esteem, but being offered help might make her upset that she appears so frail. While the golden rule provides positive guidance in general, there will always be cases when our best intentions fall foul. Such instances should not discourage us from using the golden rule, but they do show us one of its limitations.

More serious is the weight we attach to our values versus someone else's. Suppose your friend really wants to do a bungee jump. You consider leaping 200ft off a bridge to be very dangerous and reckless, but even though you have talked extensively to your friend about your concerns they still wish to do the jump. Applying the golden rule you might think, 'My friend could die doing this jump. If I was in danger of dying then I would want to be saved. Therefore, I should do all I can to prevent my friend from doing it.' Alternatively you might think, 'My friend could die doing this jump, but this is something they really want to do. I want to be free to do what I want. Therefore, I should respect their wishes and allow them to do it.' Which route you follow depends on how you weigh up the importance of your views against your friend's. In this situation, where the chance of death is in reality fairly remote, most people would probably choose the latter option. But if you knew the company he wanted to jump with had a particularly bad accident record, you would be more inclined to follow the former line of thought. There is no clear-cut way of deciding how much importance to give to your views relative to anyone else's; all you can do is try to balance the two as best you can. Yet despite the difficulties of applying the golden rule, it is still very useful as a moral guide. By asking us to be informed in our judgements and consider people other than ourselves it encourages us to adopt a less prejudiced, more equitable attitude.[89]

(Q12) Is a subjective purpose to life depressing?

Some might find the idea that we are free to find our own meaning in life rather vacuous. How can you win a game of football unless there are some rules to play by? I take the opposite view and think that the ability to choose your own meaning in life is a magnificent thing. If there were some objective purpose to life it would be very depressing if you realised you had no hope of achieving it and even if you did accomplish it, there would be nothing left to live for after that. Choosing your own meaning, on the other hand, gives every person the opportunity to live a worthwhile life, regardless of when, where, and by whom they are born.

(Q13) Is it possible for more than one theory of value to cohere with all of the available evidence?

Evidence coheres when it fits together consistently and is mutually explanatory. As such, there may be more than one theory which contains cohering evidence. The best theory, however, will explain the most evidence. Therefore, the theory of value which explains the most available evidence will be the most probable. The theory I have outlined is my own view, but you may interpret the evidence differently. Whether you agree with me or not, it is important that all of us be prepared to alter our opinions on the basis of new evidence. If we do not, we risk holding on to improbable and outdated beliefs.

In this chapter I have laid out some basic objections to my theory and responses. The discussion has necessarily veered into the realm of morality, without which the subject cannot be fully explored. There is a lot more that could be said, though, and you are free to disagree with some, possibly all, of what I have written. Regardless of your judgement, however, I hope to have shown the value of critically assessing ones views. We can test the validity of our judgements by seeking justifications for each claim we make and then requiring further justifications for each answer. In doing so we delve deeper into our theories and are better able to assess how well they account for the available evidence. Only by undertaking such a process can we be satisfied that our opinions are supported by sound reasoning.

8

Conclusion

There is a popular myth that in order to lead a meaningful life you must be a sad and tortured individual. Many of the best composers, writers and philosophers are frequently portrayed as people emotionally crippled by their quest to render purpose in their lives through their genius. Regardless of the factual accuracy of such life histories, they do raise an important question: are some types of happiness more preferable than others? Is it better, for instance, to lead a meaningful life featuring little types one and two happiness?

It is undoubtedly the case that in some circumstances achieving an increase in type two happiness requires taking a cut in type one. For example, enjoying the satisfaction of gaining a degree will mean, at least temporarily, reducing the number of hours spent in the pub or partying. It is not for me, though, to dictate that one type of happiness is better than another or what the best balance between them is. People have to make their own choice about which, in different situations, they believe is more worthwhile.

It is important to recognise, though, that pursuing types one and two happiness can be compatible with developing type three. There are some who argue, using the gene-centred view of evolution briefly described in chapter 2, that if we are merely vehicles through which our genes seek to replicate themselves, then many of what we take to be our natural desires are actually impulses that have evolved to benefit our genes. Following this argument, they claim that when we act to feel happier all we are doing is following the plan laid out by our genes. Admittedly, if we act with an understanding of our inbuilt desires and make our own decisions we are manipulating the genetic programming rather than obeying it, but we are still operating within a system of punishment and reward structured by our genetic coding. Proponents of this argument claim that only when we pursue type three happiness do we break away from the rules created by our genes. In chapters 6 and 7, however, we have seen that leading a meaningful life need not necessarily involve turning your back on the first two types of happiness. Appreciating experience is perfectly compatible with enjoying pleasures and feeling content. Regardless of whether you agree with this idea or not, **it is of crucial importance to define your own life meaning.** If you only ever adopt other people's values rather than determine your own, you risk making choices that one day, in a moment of clarity, you come to be utterly disappointed with.

Even if we do follow our own values, we should also be prepared for things going wrong. Every decision we make has a chance of success and a chance of failure. We can work to bring probability in our favour, but even with the best effort people still get divorced, lose their jobs and suffer other calamities. When pursuing our own goals all we can do is try our hardest and deal with the consequences as best we can. While the advice of this book may be useful in handling many situations, it by no means provides an infallible guide. Life is far too rich and varied for any advice to be appropriate in all circumstances. Please take what has been said here as a series of thoughtful suggestions from which you may accept some and disregard others.

The last of these is to be wary of assessing how happy you are too frequently. Although some self-analysis is useful, too much can impede happiness. Rather than repeatedly filling out positivity questionnaires or perpetually asking yourself why you exist, your time would be far better spent embracing life's experiences – enjoy the moment. By relishing what we have, we make the most of the endlessly incredible experience we have been gifted.

Appendix: The Science of Happiness

As much of the evidence in this book comes from scientific experiments, it is worth giving a brief account of how psychologists go about studying happiness. The traditional way to investigate hedonics (the science of happiness) was to ask people in one-off surveys how they felt about themselves. A typical question might be, 'All things considered, how satisfied are you with your life as a whole?' This may seem like the most obvious way of going about assessing type two happiness, but there are actually some substantial defects with this approach:

1. Such surveys are very sensitive to the immediate feelings of the respondent. One study was engineered such that immediately before subjects answered questions about life satisfaction some of them found a dime. Participants who had just found the coin reported higher satisfaction with their entire lives than those that had not.[90]

2. A person's response to how happy they are depends to a large extent on who they compare themselves against. I am much more likely to be satisfied with my lot when I compare myself to someone suffering from severe deprivation than a work colleague.

3. People do not like to admit to others, or themselves, that they are not happy, which is why people report higher levels of well-being in face-to-face interviews than postal studies.[91]

Luckily there are some antidotes to these problems. The experience sampling method is a technique which has risen in prominence in the field. This type of investigation involves participants providing multiple responses to questions over a period of time. This allows one-off jumps or dips in happiness to be averaged out. There is still the issue, however, of separating correlation from causation. In a well-known example from the medical world, numerous studies showed that women who were taking hormone replacement therapy (HRT) had a lower-than-average incidence of coronary heart disease. This led doctors to propose that HRT helped protect against coronary heart disease. Re-analysis of the data, though, showed that women undertaking HRT were more likely to be from higher socio-economic groups and therefore have better than average diets and exercise regimes. When later studies were conducted which filtered this effect out, it was found that HRT actually caused a small increase in the risk of developing coronary heart disease.[92] This example shows the importance of adequately controlling potentially significant variables when conducting experiments. Doing so means the underlying cause of a variation can be found rather than one which happens to correlate. In psychology research this is normally done by having a control group who undergo exactly the same procedures as the experimental group except for the one factor which is to be tested. Much like the HRT studies, though, it is possible for an inappropriate control group to invalidate psychology experiments. Having said this, when several large and well controlled psychology studies deliver the same conclusions, we can place a reasonable amount of faith in them.

The purpose of relating these issues has not been to make you distrust happiness research, but to highlight that there are some underlying issues to be aware of. Evidence from a scientific study can be given a lot more credence than the story of an individual but although the results of a single small experiment may be a useful starting point, they should not be taken as gospel. Unfortunately, because the scientific study of happiness is in its infancy, there are many areas in which more research is needed to provide us with greater assurance of current findings. As a result, while it is reasonable to try the recommendations of existing studies, the limitations of the evidence should make us both wary of placing too much reliance on their advice and also give us more confidence in challenging findings with which our personal experience conflicts.

Further Reading

Happiness

Nettle, D. (2005) *Happiness: The Science Behind Your Smile* New York: Oxford University Press. A good introduction to the scientific study of happiness.

Lyubomirsky, S. (2007) *The How of Happiness: A Practical Approach to Getting the Life You Want* London: Sphere. A well researched guide to happiness.

Csikszentmihalyi, M. (2002) *Flow: The Classic Work on How to Achieve Happiness* London: Rider. The best introduction to flow from the man who invented the concept.

Seligman, M. (2003) *Authentic Happiness* London: Nicholas Brealey.

Diener, E. and Biswas-Diener, R (2008) *Happiness: Unlocking the Mysteries of Psychological Wealth* Oxford: Wiley-Blackwell.

www.worlddatabaseofhappiness.eur.nl The premier register of scientific research on happiness.

Philosophy

Russell, B. (2nd ed. 1998) *The Problems of Philosophy* Oxford: Oxford University Press. A classic which focuses on the philosophy of knowledge.

Popkin, R. and Stroll, A. (2nd ed. 1986) *Philosophy Made Simple* Oxford: Made Simple Books. A very good introduction to all areas of philosophy.

Baggini, J. (2004) *What's It All About?: Philosophy and the Meaning of Life* London: Granta Books. An accessible investigation into what can give life meaning.

Nagel, T. (1987) *What Does It All Mean?: A Very Short Introduction to Philosophy* New York: Oxford University Press. Provides a short look at the main questions philosophy seeks to address.

Kiernan-Lewis, D. (2000) *Learning to Philosophize: A Primer* Belmont: Wadsworth. A short introduction which looks at how to think about philosophical problems.

Pojman, L. (3rd ed. 1999) *Ethics: Discovering Right and Wrong* Belmont: Wadsworth Publishing Company. A clear introduction to the philosophy of morality and different ethical theories.

Gensler, H. (1998) *Ethics: A Contemporary Introduction* London: Routledge. A clear introduction to different ethical theories including an excellent chapter on the golden rule.

Thompson, M. (2003) *Teach Yourself Eastern Philosophy* London: Teach Yourself A very accessible introduction to the major schools of eastern thought.

Morton, A. (3rd ed. 2002) *A Guide Through the Theory of Knowledge* Oxford: Blackwell. Together with Russell's book, the best introduction to the philosophy of knowledge.

www.nigelwarburton.typepad.com/philosophy_bites Podcasts of major philosophers interviewed on a wide range of topics.

Evolutionary Psychology

Dawkins, R. (3rd ed. 2006) *The Selfish Gene* New York: Oxford University Press. Dawkins' overtly anti-religious stance in some of his writings can put readers off, but he tones it down in this book. Well worth reading if you have not already done so.

Buss, D. (3rd ed. 2008) *Evolutionary Psychology: The New Science of the Mind* Boston: Allyn and Bacon. An excellent introduction to evolutionary psychology that I cannot recommend enough.

Meditation

Bodian, S. (2nd ed. 2006) *Meditation for Dummies* Indianapolis: Wiley Publishing. Covers the basics of meditation from both a practical and spiritual perspective.

Hanh, T. (1995) *Peace is Every Step: The Path of Mindfulness in Everyday Life* London: Rider.

Nutrition

www.eatwell.gov.uk A reliable resource for basic information on a healthy diet. For more detail see Food Standards Agency (11th ed. 2008) *Manual of Nutrition* Norwich: The Stationary Office.

Sleep

Horne, J. (2006) *Sleepfaring: A Journey Through the Science of Sleep* Oxford: Oxford University Press. A lay guide to the scientific study of sleep. Includes useful advice for those with sleeping difficulties.

Notes

1. De Maistre, X. (2004) *A Journey Around My Room* London: Hesperus Press, p. 37.

2. De Botton, A. (2003) *The Art of Travel* London: Penguin, p. 246.

3. Easterlin, R. (1995) 'Will Raising the Incomes of All Increase the Happiness of All?' *Journal of Economic Behaviour*, 27, pp. 35-47; Layard, R. (2005) *Happiness: Lessons From a New Science* London: Allen Lane, p. 29-30.

4. Seligman, M. (2003) *Authentic Happiness* London: Nicholas Brealey, p. 117.

5. Both Diener and Seligman do mention it in Diener, E. and Biswas-Diener, R (2008) *Happiness: Unlocking the Mysteries of Psychological Wealth* Oxford: Wiley-Blackwell and Seligman, M. (2003) *Authentic Happiness* London: Nicholas Brealey. Their reticence to expand on it is probably because they are both professional psychologists and this area is more the domain of philosophy than science.

6. Stubbe, J., Posthuma, D., Boosma, D. and De Geus, E. (2005) 'Heritability of Life Satisfaction in Adults: A Twin-Family Study' *Psychological Medicine* 35, pp. 1581-8; Kohler, H., Behrman, J. and Skytthe, A. (2005) 'Partner + Children = Happiness? The Effects of Partnerships and Fertility on Well-Being' *Population and Development Review* 31, pp. 407-45; Lykken, D. and Tellegen, A. (1996) 'Happiness is a stochastic phenomenon' *Psychological Science* 7, pp. 186-9; Lucas, R. and Donnellan, M. (2007) 'How Stable is Happiness? Using the STARTS Model to Estimate the Stability of Life Satisfaction' *Journal of Research in Personality* 41, pp. 1091-98; Tellegen, A., Lykken, D., Bouchard, T., Wilcox, J., Segal, L. and Rich, S. (1988) 'Personality Similarity in Twins Reared Apart and Together' *Journal of Personality and Social Psychology* 54, pp. 1031-9; Nes, R., Roysamb, E., Tambs, K., Harris, J. and Reichborn-Kjennerud, T. (2006) *Psychological Medicine* 36, pp. 1033-42.

7. Dawkins, R. (3rd ed. 2006) *The Selfish Gene* New York: Oxford University Press.

8. Sapolsky, R. (1998) *Why Zebras Don't Get Ulcers: An Updated Guide to Stress, Stress-Related Diseases, and Coping* New York: W H Freeman, p.10.

9. Riis, J., Loewenstein, G., Baron, J., Jepson, C., Fagerlin, A. and Ubel, P. (2005) 'Ignorance of Hedonic Adaptation to Hemodialysis: A Study Using Ecological Momentary Assessment' *Journal of Experimental Psychology: General*, 134, pp. 3-9.

10. For noise pollution see Weinstein, N. (1982) 'Community Noise Problems: Evidence Against Adaptation' *Journal of Environmental Psychology* 2, pp. 87-97. For widowhood see Lucas, R., Clark, A., Georgellis, Y. and Diener, E. (2003) 'Re-examining Adaptation and the Set Point Model of Happiness: Reactions to Changes in Marital Status' *Journal of Personality and Social Psychology* 84, pp. 527-39; Frederick, S. and Loewenstein, G. (1999) 'Hedonic Adaptation' in Kahneman,

D., Diener, E. and Schwarz, N. eds. (1999) *Well-Being: The Foundations of Hedonic Psychology* New York: Russell Stage Foundation, pp. 302-29.

11. Kahneman, D., Krueger, A., Schkade, D., Schwarz, N. and Stone, A. (2004) 'A Survey Method for Characterizing Daily Life Experience: The Day Reconstruction Model' *Science* 306, p. 1778.

12. Lyubomirsky, S. and Tkach, C. (2004) 'The Consequences of Dysphoric Rumination' in Papageorgiou, C. and Wells, A. eds. (2004) *Depressive Rumination: Nature, Theory and Treatment* Chichester: John Wiley and Sons, pp. 21-41; Nolen-Hoeksema, S. (2003) *Women Who Think Too Much* London: Judy Piatkus, pp. 3-31.

13. McCullough, M. and Witvliet, C. (2002) 'The Psychology of Forgiveness' in Snyder, C. and Lopez, S. eds. (2002) *Handbook of Positive Psychology* New York: Oxford University Press pp. 446-58; McCullough, M. (2001) 'Forgiveness: Who Does It and How Do They Do It?' *Current Directions in Psychological Science* 10, pp. 194-7; Hebl, J. and Enright, R. (1993) 'Forgiveness as a Psychotherapeutic Goal With Elderly Females' *Psychotherapy: Theory, Research, Practice, Training* 30, pp. 658-67.

14. Easterlin, R. (1995) 'Will Raising the Incomes of All Increase the Happiness of All?' *Journal of Economic Behaviour*, 27, pp. 35-47; Layard, R. (2005) *Happiness: Lessons From a New Science* London: Allen Lane, p. 29-30

15. White, A. (2007) 'A Global Projection of Subjective Well-being: A Challenge To Positive Psychology?' *Psychtalk* 56, pp. 17-20.

16. Nettle, D. (2005) *Happiness: The Science Behind Your Smile* New York: Oxford University Press, p. 72; Layard, R. (2005) *Happiness: Lessons From a New Science* London: Allen Lane, p. 32; Diener, E. and Biswas-Diener, R (2008) *Happiness: Unlocking the Mysteries of Psychological Wealth* Oxford: Wiley-Blackwell, pp. 105-9.

17. Such concern is not a recent phenomenon. The *British Medical Journal* editorial of 29 September 1894 (p. 719) proclaims that 'the hurry and excitement of modern life is quite correctly held to be responsible for much of the insomnia of which we hear; and most of the articles and letters are full of good advice to live more quietly and of platitudes concerning the harmfulness of rush and worry. The pity of it is that so many people are unable to follow this good advice and are obliged to lead a life of anxiety and high tension.'

18. Horne, J. (2006) *Sleepfaring: A Journey Through the Science of Sleep* Oxford: Oxford University Press, p. 188.

19. Horne, J. (2006) *Sleepfaring: A Journey Through the Science of Sleep* Oxford: Oxford University Press, p. 102.

20. Horne, J. (2006) *Sleepfaring: A Journey Through the Science of Sleep* Oxford: Oxford University Press, pp. 177-85; Horne, J., Anderson, C. and Platten, C. (2008) 'Sleep Extension Versus Nap or Coffee, Within the Context of Sleep Debt' *Journal of Sleep Research*, 17, pp. 432-6.

21. Kripke, D., Garfinkel, L., Wingard, D., Klauber, M. and Marler, M. (2002) 'Mortality Associated With Sleep Duration and Insomnia' *Archives of General Psychiatry* 59, pp. 131-6; Tamakoshi, A. and Ohno, Y. (2004) 'Self-Reported Sleep Duration as a Predictor of All-Cause Mortality: Results from the JACC study, Japan' *Sleep* 27, pp. 51-4; Ayas, N., White, D., Manson, J., Stampfer, M., Speizer, F., Malhotra, A. and Hu, F. (2003) 'A Prospective Study of Sleep Duration and Coronary Heart Disease in Women' *Archives of Internal Medicine* 163, pp. 205-9.

22. For a succinct overview of both sides of this debate see Dinges, D. (2004) 'Sleep Debt and Scientific Evidence' *Sleep* 27, pp. 1050-2; Horne, J. (2004) 'Is There a Sleep Debt?' *Sleep* 27, pp. 1047-9.

23. Horne, J. (2006) *Sleepfaring: A Journey Through the Science of Sleep* Oxford: Oxford University Press, p. 36-38, 179.

24. For crisps see Coghlan, A. (22 April 2006) 'Acrylamide: The Food Scare the World Forgot' *New Scientist* 2548. For an analysis of the possible benefits of fish oil and pomegranates see Goldacre, B. (2008) *Bad Science* London: Fourth Estate, pp. 88 and 136-60.

25. Goldacre, B. (2008) *Bad Science* London: Fourth Estate, p. 129.

26. Food Standards Agency (11th ed. 2008) *Manual of Nutrition* Norwich: The Stationary Office.

27. Food Standards Agency (11th ed. 2008) *Manual of Nutrition* Norwich: The Stationary Office, p. 114.

28. Expert Group on Vitamins and Minerals (2003) *Safe Upper Levels for Vitamins and Minerals*, available at: www.food.gov.uk/multimedia/pdfs/vitmin2003.pdf

29. Gesch, B. (2005) 'The potential of nutrition to promote physical and behavioural well-being' in Huppert, F., Baylis, N. and Keverne, B. eds. *The Science of Well-Being* Oxford: Oxford University Press, pp. 171-214.

30. Processed food is likely to contain higher levels of saturated fat and salt than fresh produce, and it will probably have lost some nutrients during processing

31. Emmons, R. and McCullough, M. (2003) 'Counting Blessings Versus Burdens: An Experimental Investigation of Gratitude and Subjective Well-Being in Daily Life' *Journal of Personality and Social Psychology* 84, pp. 377-389. Other studies which show a connection between appreciating experience and happiness are Seligman, M., Rashid, T. and Parks, A. (2006) 'Positive Psychotherapy' *American Psychologist* 61, pp. 774-88 and Brown, K. and Ryan, R. (2003) 'The Benefits of Being Present: Mindfulness and its Role in Psychological Well-Being' *Journal of Personality and Social Psychology* 84, pp. 822-848.

32. Lyubomirsky, S. (2007) *The How of Happiness: A Practical Approach to Getting the Life You Want* London: Sphere, pp. 90-1.

33. St Augustine (1972) *The City of God* (trans. Bettenson, H.) London: Penguin Books, p. 970.

34. Hanh, T. (1995) *Peace is Every Step: The Path of Mindfulness in Everyday Life* London: Rider pp. 21-2 and 26.

35. Bryant, F., Smart, C. and King, S. (2005) 'Using the Past to Enhance the Present: Boosting Happiness Through Positive Reminiscence' *Journal of Happiness Studies*, 6, pp. 227-260.

36. Lyubomirsky, S. (2007) *The How of Happiness: A Practical Approach to Getting the Life You Want* London: Sphere, p. 130.

37. Lyubomirsky, S., Sheldon, K. and Schkade, D. (2005) 'Pursuing Happiness: The Architecture of Sustainable Change' *Review of General Psychology* 9, pp. 111-31; Lyubomirsky, S. (2007) *The How of Happiness: A Practical Approach to Getting the Life You Want* London: Sphere, pp. 128-9.

38. Admittedly, in some situations (e.g. working in a hospital) empathy has to be restrained in order to operate effectively. Most of the time, however, developing greater empathy is beneficial to all concerned.

39. Remnick, D. (18 Sept. 2006) 'The Wanderer' *New Yorker*.

40. Lyubomirsky, S. and Tkach, C. (2004) 'The Consequences of Dysphoric Rumination' in Papageorgiou, C. and Wells, A. eds. (2004) *Depressive Rumination: Nature, Theory and Treatment* Chichester: John Wiley and Sons, pp. 21-41; Nolen-Hoeksema, S. (2003) *Women Who Think Too Much* London: Judy Piatkus, pp. 3-31.

41. Lyubomirsky, S. (2007) *The How of Happiness: A Practical Approach to Getting the Life You Want* London: Sphere, pp. 119-23.

42. Layard, R. (2005) *Happiness: Lessons From a New Science* London: Allen Lane, pp. 195-7.

43. Hicks, J. and Allen, G. (1999) *A Century of Change: Trends in UK Statistics Since 1900* House of Commons Library Research Paper 99/111, available at: www.parliament.uk/parliamentary_publications_and_archives/research_papers/research_papers_1999.cfm

44. Godfrey, B., Williams, C. and Lawrence, P. (2008) *History and Crime* London: Sage, p. 31.

45. Godfrey, B., Williams, C. and Lawrence, P. (2008) *History and Crime* London: Sage, p. 32.

46. Homicide data taken from www.ons.gov.uk/ons/rel/crime-stats/crime-statistics/period-ending-march-2013/sty-crime-in-england-and-wales.html 0.0001% represents the annual chance of being a victim of homicide using 2012 homicide and population figures.

47. The FBI recorded 14,827 murders in the USA in 2012 (www.fbi.gov/about-us/cjis/ucr/crime-in-the-u.s/2012/crime-in-the-u.s.-2012/violent-crime/murder). 19,656 deaths were due to falls in the USA in 2005 (the latest publicly available data). See National Safety Council *The Odds of Dying From...*, available at: www.nsc.org/research/odds.aspx

48. There were 1,815 deaths due to transport accidents in England and Wales in 2011 (the latest publicly available data). See Office for National Statistics *Mortality Statistics: Deaths Registered in 2011*, available at: www.ons.gov.uk/ons/rel/vsob1/mortality-statistics--deaths-registered-in-england-and-wales--series-dr-/2011/index.html. There were 45,343 deaths due to motor-vehicle accidents in the USA in 2005. See National Safety Council *The Odds of Dying From...*, available at: www.nsc.org/research/odds.aspx

49. Mueller, J. (2005) 'Six Rather Unusual Propositions About Terrorism' *Terrorism and Political Violence*, 17, p. 488.

50. Schwartz, B., Ward, A., Lyubomirsky, S., Monterosso, J., White, K. and Lehman, D. (2002) 'Maximizing Versus Satisficing: Happiness is a Matter of Choice' *Journal of Personality and Social Psychology* 83, pp. 1178-97.

51. For reviews of the vast literature see Kruk, J. (2007) 'Physical Activity in the Prevention of the Most Frequent Chronic Diseases: an Analysis of the Recent Evidence' *Asian Pacific Journal of Cancer Prevention* 8, pp. 325-38; Warburton, D., Nicol, C. and Bredin, S. (2006) 'Health Benefits of Physical Activity: The Evidence' *Canadian Medical Association Journal* 174 (6), pp. 801-9; Blair, S., Kohl, H. and Gordon, N. (1992) 'How Much Physical Activity is Good for Health?' *Annual Review of Public Health* 13, pp. 99-126.

52. For reviews see Biddle, S. and Ekkekakis, P. (2005) 'Physically Active Lifestyles and Well-Being' in Huppert, F., Baylis, N. and Keverne, B. eds. (2005) *The Science of Well-Being* Oxford: Oxford University Press; Biddle, S. (2000) 'Emotion, Mood, and Physical Activity' in Biddle, S., Fox, K. and Boutcher, S. eds. (2000) *Physical Activity and Psychological Well-Being* London: Routledge, pp. 63-87.

53. For a review see Spector, P. (1997) *Job Satisfaction: Application, Assessment, Cause and Consequences* London: Sage, pp. 50-1.

54. Wrzesniewski, A. and Dutton, J. (2001) 'Crafting a Job: Revisioning Employees as Active Crafters of Their Work' *Academy of Management Review* 26, pp. 179-201.

55. Wrzesniewski, A., McCauley, C., Rozin, P. and Scwartz, B. (1997) 'Jobs, Careers and Callings: People's Relations to Their Work' *Journal of Research in Personality* 31, pp. 21-33.

56. Perhaps the best book on 'flow' is Csikszentmihalyi, M. (2002) *Flow: The Classic Work on How to Achieve Happiness* London: Rider.

57. It is this subsequent feeling of enjoyment which leads me to consider flow as a combination of type one and two happiness rather than type three.

58. Csikszentmihalyi, M. (2002) *Flow: The Classic Work on How to Achieve Happiness* London: Rider, p. 39.

59. Csikszentmihalyi, M. (2002) *Flow: The Classic Work on How to Achieve Happiness* London: Rider, pp. 158-161.

60. Sapolsky, R. (1998) *Why Zebras Don't Get Ulcers: An Updated Guide to Stress, Stress-Related Diseases, and Coping* New York: W H Freeman, p.10-12.

61. For a review see Shapiro, S., Schwartz, G. and Santerre, C. (2002) 'Meditation and Positive Psychology' in Snyder, C. and Lopez, S. eds. (2002) *Handbook of Positive Psychology* New York: Oxford University Press, pp. 632-45.

62. This breathing meditation is adapted from Hanh, T. (1995) *Peace is Every Step: The Path of Mindfulness in Everyday Life* London: Rider, p. 8.

63. Diener, E. and Biswas-Diener, R (2008) *Happiness: Unlocking the Mysteries of Psychological Wealth* Oxford: Wiley-Blackwell, p. 93.

64. Frank, R. (1999) *Luxury Fever: Why Money Fails to Satisfy in an Era of Excess* New York: The Free Press, pp. 111-21; Spector, P. (1997) *Job Satisfaction: Application, Assessment, Cause and Consequences* London: Sage, p. 42. Interestingly, social status may explain why it has been found that homeless people in India are happier than their counter-parts in the USA. As poverty is far more widespread in India than the USA the homeless of the former country may not regard their social standing as negatively as those of the latter do. See Biswas-Diener, R. and Diener, E. (2006) 'The Subjective Well-Being of the Homeless and Lessons for Happiness' *Social Indicators Research*, 76, pp. 185-205. Also worthy of note is the finding that increased social status may be the reason that, despite the occasional horror story reported in the press, most lottery winners become lastingly happier as a result of their windfall. See Gardner, J. and Oswald, A. (2007) 'Money and Mental Well-Being: A Longitudinal Study of Medium-Sized Lottery Wins' *Journal of Health Economics* 26, pp. 49-60 (n.b. An older study (Brickman, P., Coates, D. and Janoff-Bulman, R. (1978) 'Lottery Winners and Accident Victims: Is Happiness Relative?' *Journal of Personality and Social Psychology* 36, pp. 917-27) claimed that winning the lottery produces no lasting increase in happiness because people adapt to their fortune, but unlike Gardner and Oswald's study it did not follow subjects over time and used a much smaller sample).

65. Easterlin, R. (1995) 'Will Raising the Incomes of All Increase the Happiness of All?' *Journal of Economic Behaviour*, 27, pp. 35-47; Layard, R. (2005) *Happiness: Lessons From a New Science* London: Allen Lane, p. 29-30.

66. Mencken, H. (1949) *A Mencken Chrestomathy* New York: Alfred A Knopf, p. 619.

67. Buss, D. (2nd ed. 2004) *Evolutionary Psychology: The New Science of the Mind* London: Pearson, pp. 114-5.

68. Lyubomirsky, S. and Ross, L. (1997) 'Hedonic Consequences of Social Comparison: A Contrast of Happy and Unhappy People' *Journal of Personality and Social Psychology* 73, pp. 1141-57.

69. Seligman, M. (2003) *Authentic Happiness* London: Nicholas Brealey, pp. 161-6.

70. Lyubomirsky, S., King, L. and Diener, E. (2005) 'The Benefits of Frequent Positive Affect: Does Happiness Lead to Success?' *Psychological Bulletin* 131, pp. 803-55; Myers, D. (2000) 'The Funds, Friends and Faith of Happy People' *American Psychologist* 55, pp. 56-67; Haring-Hidore, M., Stock, W., Okun, M. and Witter, R. (1985) 'Marital Status and Subjective Well-Being: A Research Synthesis' *Journal of Marriage and the Family* 47, pp. 947-53.

71. Dawkins, R. (3rd ed. 2006) *The Selfish Gene* New York: Oxford University Press.

72. Buss, D. (3rd ed. 2008) *Evolutionary Psychology: The New Science of the Mind* Boston: Allyn and Bacon.

73. Buss, D. (3rd ed. 2008) *Evolutionary Psychology: The New Science of the Mind* Boston: Allyn and Bacon, pp. 110-37.

74. Clarke, R. and Hatfield, E. (1989) 'Gender Differences in Receptivity to Sexual Offers' *Journal of Psychology and Human Sexuality* 2, pp. 39-55.

75. Buss, D. (2nd ed. 2004) *Evolutionary Psychology: The New Science of the Mind* London: Pearson, p. 174.

76. Kenrick, D., Neuberg, S., Zierk, K. and Krones, J. (1994) 'Evolution and Social Cognition: Contrast Effects as a Function of Sex, Dominance and Physical Attractiveness' *Personality and Social Psychology Bulletin* 20, pp. 210-7.

77. Rozin, P. and Fallon, A. (1988) 'Body Image, Attitudes to Weight and Misperceptions of Figure Preferences of the Opposite Sex: A Comparison of Men and Women in Two Generations' *Journal of Abnormal Psychology* 97, pp. 342-5.

78. Gottman, J. and Silver, N. (1999) *The Seven Principles for Making Marriage Work* London: Weidenfeld & Nicolson.

79. Goleman, D. (2004) *Emotional Intelligence: Why it Can Matter More Than IQ & Working With Emotional Intelligence* London: Bloomsbury, pp. 131-44.

80. Goleman, D. (2004) *Emotional Intelligence: Why it Can Matter More Than IQ & Working With Emotional Intelligence* London: Bloomsbury, pp. 140-1.

81. Goleman, D. (2004) *Emotional Intelligence: Why it Can Matter More Than IQ & Working With Emotional Intelligence* London: Bloomsbury, pp. 141-2.

82. Gottman, J. and Silver, N. (1999) *The Seven Principles for Making Marriage Work* London: Weidenfeld & Nicolson, p. 40.

83. Lucas, R., Clark, A., Georgellis, Y. and Diener, E. (2003) 'Re-examining Adaptation and the Set Point Model of Happiness: Reactions to Changes in Marital Status' *Journal of Personality and Social Psychology* 84, pp. 527-39.

84. Gottman, J. and Silver, N. (1999) *The Seven Principles for Making Marriage Work* London: Weidenfeld & Nicolson.

85. Descartes' famous phrase, 'I think, therefore I am,' makes the assumption that if there are thoughts then there must be a thinker. In fact, all we can be sure of is that there are thoughts.

86. If I flip a fair coin 21 times, before any coins have been thrown the probability of 21 heads is 1 in 2,097,152. The probability of flipping a head after having already flipped 20 heads in a row, however, is simply 1 in 2. The outcomes of previous flips do not alter the probability of future ones (unless a rigged coin is used!)

87. McGeer, V. (2008) 'Varieties of Moral Agency: Lessons from Autism (and Psychopathy)' in Sinnott-Armstrong, W. ed. (2008) *Moral Psychology* Cambridge:

MIT Press, 3; Kagan, J. (2008) 'Morality and its Development' in Sinnott-Armstrong, W. ed. (2008) *Moral Psychology* Cambridge: MIT Press, 3.

88. For a list of authorities (including every major world religion) who endorse the golden rule see Gensler, H. (1996) *Formal Ethics* London: Routledge, pp. 104-5.

89. Further discussion of the golden rule can be found in Gensler, H. (1998) *Ethics: A Contemporary Introduction* London: Routledge; Wattles, J. (1996) *The Golden Rule* New York: Oxford University Press; Singer, M. (2002) *The Ideal of a Rational Morality* Oxford: Clarendon; Gensler, H. (1996) *Formal Ethics* London: Routledge.

90. Schwarz, N. and Strack, N. (1999) 'Reports of Subjective Well-Being: Judgemental Processes and Their Methodological Implications' in Kahneman, D., Diener, E. and Schwarz, N. eds. (1999) *Well-Being: The Foundations of Hedonic Psychology* New York: Russell Stage Foundation pp. 61-84.

91. Smith, T. (1979) 'Happiness: Time Trends, Seasonal Variations, Intersurvey Differences and Other Mysteries' *Social Psychology Quarterly* 42, pp. 18-30.

92. Lawlor, D., Smith, G. and Ebrahim, S. (2004) 'The Hormone Replacement – Coronary Heart Disease Conundrum: Is This the Death of Observational Epidemiology?' *International Journal of Epidemiology* 33, pp. 464-7.

4633131R00051

Printed in Great Britain
by Amazon.co.uk, Ltd.,
Marston Gate.